DISASSEMBLED

A Native Son on Janesville and General Motors—
a Story of Grit, Race, Gender, and Wishful Thinking
and What it Means for America

TIM CULLEN

EDITED BY
DOUG MOE

LITTLE CREEK PRESS
AND BOOK DESIGN

Mineral Point, Wisconsin USA

✳

Little Creek Press®
A Division of Kristin Mitchell Design, Inc.
5341 Sunny Ridge Road
Mineral Point, Wisconsin 53565

Book Design and Project Coordination: Little Creek Press

First Printing September 2019

Printed in Wisconsin, United States of America

For more information or to order books: www.littlecreekpress.com

Library of Congress Control Number: 2019911899

ISBN-10: 1-942586-62-0
ISBN-13: 978-1-942586-62-3

On the cover: A picture of the end. The one-hundred-year-old smokestack from the
GM plant comes down in 2019 to join the rest of the rubble that was the plant.
Photo credit Andrew Sigwell.

All the profits from this book will go to a scholarship foundation started by the author, Tim Cullen. The Janesville Multicultural Teacher Scholarship Foundation provides scholarships of $5,000 per year for Janesville students of color who want to be teachers and agree to teach in Janesville.

Our community is like so many others that were formerly almost all white but are now much more racially diverse. Our teachers are almost all white. The goal of this scholarship is to have more diverse teachers—like the students they teach. Janesville teachers are among the strongest supporters of this foundation.

MORE PRAISE FOR DISASSEMBLED...

❝A good, comprehensive read of Janesville and the General Motors years."

—John Scott III, son or John Scott and retired Rock County Deputy Sheriff

❝I think you will find Tim's insight on the UAW's progressive platform to not create a bigger piece of the pie for its blue collar workers, but rather create a bigger pie for all American families was the key to success for our small town for many years... and how it can all suddenly change."

—Bruce Penny, past UAW Local 95 President and retired UAW International Representative

❝Through recounting the history of the Janesville General Motors plant, Tim Cullen also shares unique stories of individuals whose vision, leadership, and persistence left indelible legacies in our community and beyond. The Rock County community did not allow the closing of the GM plant define the future; indeed, it became a catalyst for new growth and hope."

—Sue Conley, Janesville City Councilwoman

TABLE OF CONTENTS

DISASSEMBLED

ABOUT THE AUTHOR

Tim Cullen was born and raised in Janesville, Wisconsin. Cullen graduated from UW-Whitewater with a Major in Political Science with a minor in History. He is the third generation of his family to work at General Motors. He worked there for four summers in the 1960s to pay his way through college. He also was involved in helping GM and the UAW as a state senator representing Janesville. Governor Jim Doyle appointed him to co-chair a task force in 2008 to try to save the plant. He has had a lifetime of connections with the "plant." The first election he won was to the Janesville City Council in 1970. Four years later Cullen was elected to the State Senate at the age of 30. He went on to become Senate Majority Leader and in 1987 he became Secretary of the Department of Health and Social Services under Governor Tommy Thompson. In 1988 Cullen took a job with Blue Cross and worked with them for the next 20 years. In 2010 he decided to run for his old Senate seat. He was elected and served until 2015. Today Cullen still lives in Janesville and spends his time working with the three foundations he started. He is also the chair of the board of Common Cause-Wisconsin.

Cullen will donate all profits from this book to the Janesville Multicultural Teachers Opportunity Fund he started in 2008. The sole purpose of the Fund is to raise money for college scholarships for Janesville students of color. The goal is to support those students who wish to become teachers and are willing to return to Janesville to teach for at least three years. ıl

AUTHOR'S NOTE

Writing a book is an adventure. To begin with it is a toy and an amusement. Then it becomes a mistress, then it becomes a master, then it becomes a tyrant. The last phase is that just as you are about to be reconciled to your servitude, you kill the monster and fling him out to the public. —Winston Churchill

L ike so many of Churchill's quotes, I love this one. I agree that writing a book is an adventure, especially in the sense that research and conversation along with people knowledgeable about the topic can inform and change the views you started with, even regarding a subject you believed you knew well.

I don't use terms like *mistress, master,* or *tyrant,* but the act of researching this book did instill in me a respect for facts and accuracy as opposed to theories and assumptions, no matter how widely held.

I promise the reader one thing. This is my best effort to write the most truthful, accurate book that I could write within a reasonable time frame. Given five or ten additional years to research, I might have unearthed more, and some of my conclusions may have been different. I hope that 10 or 20 years from now, someone might take up that challenge. Certainly more will be known about post-GM Janesville. Some of the players—politicians, union leaders, management—may be more forthcoming than they were willing to be in 2019. There is no shelf life on the truth and what it means.

Toward that end, I hope readers will take some time with the bibliography and appendix at the back of this book. The thoughts expressed and the books that helped me in my research are worth exploring in more depth.

Three times at the Janesville plant something was disassembled. The biggest was the great tragedy in the closing of the plant in 2008 and tearing it down in 2019. With the closing came the loss of 4,500 jobs, which therefore affected 4,500 families and the whole economy of Rock County.

There were two other disassemblings at the plant that were good things. One was the racism-inspired refusal to hire African-Americans from the plant's opening in 1923 until the late 1960's. The other was when in the 1960's the women working in the plant were finally paid the same as men and could work on the main assembly line.

Finally, let me acknowledge that if you are reading this book and worked at GM, I am certain you have stories about your time as an employee that are not included here. At some point I needed to end my research and start writing. I'm sure those missing stories could make another entire book. ▮▮

DISASSEMBLED

❶
The Reckoning

On a day in or around 2005, I walked into the General Motors Janesville Assembly Plant with some high school students from an internship program I'd started to help them get real-world experience. The core of the program had them working as interns in offices in the Wisconsin State Legislature in Madison, where I served for many years, but I also set up private sector meetings for them in Janesville.

That day, at the sprawling, nearly five million-square-foot GM facility, we were scheduled to see the plant manager, as well as the president of the United Auto Workers Local Union. What we really saw that day was the future.

I suspect it had such a big impact on me because it had been 40 years since I last set foot inside the plant. I was born and raised in Janesville and attended Whitewater State University (now UW–Whitewater), the first in my family to go to college. I came home to Janesville and worked in the GM plant during the summers.

It was the best-paying summer job in southern Wisconsin, and why not? When I worked there, from 1962 to 1965, the Janesville GM plant was booming. By the early 1970s, employment at the plant would swell to over 7,000. My summer job was part of a GM program for college-enrolled sons of employees—sons, it should be noted, not daughters.

The men in the Cullen family had a long history with GM, and this did not make us unique in Janesville. It was just the opposite. Thousands of Janesville families have a multigenerational story to tell about working for GM.

My great-grandfather, Thomas Cullen, worked at the Janesville Machine Company during the last half of the 1800s. Janesville Machine made farm implements. GM purchased it, along with the Samson Tractor Company, and in 1919 began making tractors under the Samson name at a new Janesville plant.

My grandfather—also Thomas Cullen—worked for Samson Tractor. In 1923, GM got out of the tractor business, which had not been a success, and began making cars in Janesville. That same year my grandfather quit the company and took a job as a janitor with the Janesville School District. Maybe he saw more job security with the school district than with a new company in town that had struggled to sell tractors. My grandfather was still the custodian at Roosevelt Elementary School when I attended kindergarten in 1949. I got a kick out of seeing him at school. He retired in 1951 at age 76.

My father, William Cullen, continued our family's relationship with GM. He was 40 when GM hired him in 1948, having earlier worked for Parker Pen, another significant Janesville employer. My dad was a great believer in unions in general and the United Auto Workers (UAW) in Janesville in particular. He was a proud UAW member until his death in 1971.

If by 2005 it had been 40 years since I'd physically been in the Janesville GM plant, it hadn't been out of mind. During my years in the state Senate, and later when I worked for Blue Cross Blue Shield, I kept attuned to the GM-Janesville relationship. The 1980s was a turbulent decade. We worked hard in the Legislature to accommodate GM and continue the viability of the Janesville plant, though by the turn of the new century it was clear the glory days of the 1950s–1970s were gone. Still, GM was producing sport utility vehicles (SUVs) at the Janesville plant into the 2000s, and the city remained cautiously optimistic.

Yet when I walked into the plant with the high school interns that day in 2005, I was shocked. It was the sheer reduction in the number of human beings. I recognized the difference in seconds. Where I once saw people, I now saw robots and somebody at a computer overseeing them. The automated assembly line was making people obsolete. Surely it happened gradually, over time, and if one had observed it that way it might not have been so shocking. I dropped in after 40 years, and let me tell you, my eyes were opened. The world had changed. The plant's total number of employees had dropped from around 7,100 in the 1970s to under 4,000 by 2005.

I did not feel unduly worried for Janesville, for I knew technology was causing upheaval at manufacturing plants across the country. And in 2005 I may have still overestimated both GM's financial vigor and its commitment to the longstanding Janesville plant. I was not alone.

When the reckoning came, it happened quickly, though on my next visit to the plant, hope was still in the air. That was February 13, 2008, less than one week before the Democratic presidential primary election in Wisconsin. Candidate Barack Obama spoke at the Janesville plant. I supported Obama, and some of my UAW friends invited me to the plant to hear the speech. Governor Jim Doyle was there and introduced me to Obama, who exhibited the kind of effortless charisma for which he's now famous.

Obama spoke from the plant's second floor, which may have been symbolic of something. The more modern GM plants have only one level for ease of logistics. And while the speech was inspiring—he said he could see a 100-year future for the plant— Obama stopped short of promising the Janesville plant would remain open.

On June 2, 2008, less than three months after Obama visited Janesville, GM announced it would close the plant by 2010. The timeline tempered that unwelcome news. We had 18 months to change their minds.

We tried. Governor Doyle appointed me co-chair of a task force charged with retaining General Motors in Janesville. My co-chair was Brad Dutcher, who that year had been elected Local 95 Union president. I thought the task force worked hard and presented GM a genuinely attractive retention package. Governor Doyle and I met with GM executives in Detroit— U.S. Representative Paul Ryan also attended—and we felt the meeting went well. We got them to say that a final decision had not yet been made.

In October 2008, four months after the first announcement, GM declared that the end was near. The last day of producing SUVs at the Janesville plant was just weeks away. The final day would be December 23.

I made a point of being there that morning. My family and I had a great deal invested in that plant, as did so many others in Janesville. It was a terribly sad day, with profound economic consequences for the city and the region, but as I stood and watched the last vehicle—a black Tahoe LTZ—being assembled,

I saw pride on the faces of the past and present GM employees who had gathered. It had been quite an 85-year ride.

Not everyone believed it was truly over. In spring 2009, Janesville received word that GM was putting the plant on standby status, a lifeline that my research revealed was never anchored in reality. In May 2018, while I was writing, demolition of the plant began.

In Amy Goldstein's excellent 2017 book, *Janesville: An American Story*, she traces what happened after the devastating plant closing, focusing on the displaced GM workers and their families.

This book, instead, seeks to take the economic and social measure of Janesville as a whole, a decade removed from the huge body blow of GM leaving. What does the future hold? What does the Janesville plant closure potentially mean for cities across the United States?

But even more than that, this book came out of my desire to better understand the how and why of what happened with the GM plant in Janesville. With the plant now being demolished, it's time to tell that story, how the city and state tried to keep the plant, who helped, who didn't, and what was really happening with GM as opposed to what people thought was happening.

That was my goal, and I hope I've done that story justice. But as sometimes happens when you're researching and writing, I also began looking at issues like race and gender equity, and found myself drawn to the stories of some individuals who didn't play a direct role in the plant closing and the 1984–2008 time period that's central to the book, but were important to GM and Janesville, nonetheless. In short, I found some heroes. So along with a nod to my family in the early pages, you'll find accounts of Doris Thom, who in 1965 became the first woman to work on the GM assembly line in Janesville; John Scott, Jr., the third black person hired at Janesville GM in 1961 after many years of unsuccessfully applying; and, finally, Walter Reuther, UAW International president from 1946 until his death in a plane crash in 1970, and to my mind the greatest American labor leader of the 20th century. The UAW Local 95 hall is named for Reuther, and the road that connected the Janesville GM plant to the interstate highway was named Reuther Way. The light from these three individuals still shines. ▮▮

❷
Growing Up in GM's Janesville

I grew up during the 1950s and '60s when the Janesville GM plant was referred to by most people as simply "the plant." When you heard that phrase everyone knew what it meant, despite there being other significant factories in the city— Parker Pen, Hough Shade, Gilman, and more. In those days the plant was divided into two divisions of General Motors: Fisher Body Division and Chevrolet Division. The plant assembled only Chevrolet vehicles.

The two divisions were in the same building but were quite different operations and separated by a wall. The workers at the plant were known by whether they worked at Fisher Body or at the Chevy plant. There were two different UAW unions with different union presidents: Local 95 on the Fisher Body side and Local 121 on the Chevy side. They merged into one union in 1969, and even though there were more workers to vote on the Chevrolet side, the merged union was named Local 95. This merger was at the urging of the UAW International Union and was decided by vote of the entire membership.

Over the decades these distinctions faded away, and GM officially named it GMAD for General Motors Assembly Division. People referred to it as "the GM plant" or still "the plant." GM was a dominant presence in Janesville life. GM families had stable household incomes—very much middle class.

My family was one of them, and I will take a moment here to tell you about them. In my 2015 book, *Ringside Seat*—a critical look at the administration of Wisconsin Governor Scott Walker—I gave a brief description of my older brother, Tom. He was my only sibling and two years older than me. Tom was the kindest, most gentle older brother that any younger brother could ask for. As an adult, he had a successful career as an electrician and has been married to Carole for 55 years. They have three sons: Brian, Todd, and Tim.

It deeply mattered to my dad that he was Irish, Catholic, and a Democrat. This included who he became friends with, who he and my mother socialized with, who he did business with (including his lawyer, favored gas station, retailers, and the tavern where he stopped), and, of course, who he married and how he voted.

My father died in 1971, and I miss him to this day. There is so much I wish I could talk to him about. I have often wished I had asked him how he ranked those three factors in order of importance. The following story will provide a partial answer.

When I was in college and interested in politics, I asked my dad if he had ever voted for a Republican. He said yes, he had voted for Senator Joe McCarthy, the Wisconsin senator from 1947 to 1957 best known today for abusively destroying federal government employees' reputations by accusing them of being communist or associating with communists. McCarthy's behavior as a committee chairman was nationally televised (the source of news and information in the 1950s). The hearings where he berated victims became known as the Army-McCarthy hearings. His behavior was so outrageous that the United States Senate censured him in 1954, a highly rare action taken by the Senate against one of its own.

When my dad told me he had voted for Joe McCarthy, I was stunned. I asked him, "Dad, how could you vote for Joe McCarthy?"

He looked at me and said two words: "Irish Catholic."

I then said, "Well, okay, you voted for him the first time in 1946, but not again in 1952 after all of his antics." He said yes, he did. So I asked, "Why?"

He looked at me like he felt he'd raised a son who didn't catch on very quickly. He then answered: "Irish Catholic!" This discussion answered part of my "order of importance" question. Clearly, being a Democrat ranked third.

All the Irish he knew were Catholic, but not all the Catholics he knew were Irish. So sometimes he did business with a Catholic who was not Irish if an Irish Catholic was not available. I have concluded that my dad put Irish and Catholic in a tie for first and Democrat third on his priority list. During my dad's lifetime, 1908–1971, I do not think he knew any Irish who were not Catholic.

I am convinced my dad made these choices in his life because it was his comfort zone. He grew up in the heavily Irish Fourth Ward in Janesville. The Catholic church was, you guessed it, St. Patrick's Church.

I must make clear that my dad did work with and do business with people he liked and respected who were none of the three. I believe that an Irish Catholic born in 1908 grew up at a time when Irish Catholics still stuck together as stories of discrimination against them were passed down by their elders.

My dad also believed in unions, including the UAW at GM. But he also had no inherent dislike of people in management. He respected management people who treated workers respectfully. I remember he liked several, but those he especially liked were Jack Hughes, Mike Dooley, and Ken Cummins—all Irish Catholics. I don't know what their politics were.

In the 1930s my dad was a teamster, the second person in Janesville to join that union, while he drove a truck for Gray's Beverage. He was a beer truck driver when he met my mother, Margaret, and they began dating. My mother's mom was a strict Victorian and frowned at her daughter keeping company with a beer truck driver. My dad thought fast and asked Gray's to put him on a soda truck, which they did. The relationship was saved. Six months after they were married, he was back on the beer truck.

My mother was born in 1904. She lived to 100, dying in 2004. I want to tell some stories about this wonderful woman. She was a devoted Catholic. Mother was 16 years old before women could vote for president. She was only 20 in 1924 (voting age in 1924 was 21), so she could not vote for president until 1928, at the age of 24. She was, like my dad, heavily influenced by people's religion (Catholic), nation of origin (Ireland), and politics (Democrat).

Her first vote for president, in 1928, was for Al Smith. He was three for three on my mother's priority list. She told me in 2000 when she was 96 that she had voted for the Democratic presidential candidate in every election from 1928 to 1996. We were talking in 2000 because she wanted to vote for Al Gore, the Democratic candidate, but through her involvement in the anti-abortion organization she was greatly bothered by her understanding of Gore's position on the issue of partial birth abortion. In the end, she told me that she could not vote for Gore, but could not bring herself to vote for the Republican candidate, George W. Bush. So at age 96 she solved her dilemma by voting for Ralph Nader, the Green Party candidate. I was so proud of her for caring enough about the value of her one vote for president and for how she worked it out in a way that was right for her. I believe millions of Americans go through similar serious thinking about who will get their vote.

My mother was a lifelong devoted Catholic. She never missed Sunday Mass and attended many other services. For decades she counted the collection money after Sunday Masses. She was a charter member of the Janesville Catholic Women's Club (1921), which she joined with her mother. She was anti-abortion. I voted the pro-choice position when I was in the Legislature not because I "believed" in abortions or wanted to encourage them. My view was simply that women make that decision, not politicians who are voting in a politicized environment rather than a moral environment.

My mother never talked with me about the abortion issue, even though she knew how I voted or *because* she knew how I voted, until one time very late in her life. She had been reading some stories about legislative action on the issue. She put the paper down and said to me, "I just wish the government would stay out of this abortion issue." I looked at her and said, "Mother, what you just said is exactly how I feel about the issue." She looked at me with a kind look, like she just figured out that her son was not a "murderer" as some of the literature she received portrayed legislators who voted as I did. It was a warm moment for both of us.

My mother fought depression issues for most of her adult life. She suffered through awful electric shock treatments in the 1940s and '50s, if not even earlier. She also was helped by the more humane treatments in the 1980s and '90s called ECTs (electroconvulsive therapy).

I saw the depressing effects on her when I was an adult. It made me realize what a brave, strong, loving mother Tom and I had because neither of us can ever remember our mother not being kind to us, getting up to make our breakfast, actually all meals. She had to will herself to do her "job" despite how incredibly difficult that had to have been during those times she was suffering a bout with depression.

My father died of a heart attack in 1971 at the age of 63. My mother lived to be 100. The amazing and wonderful thing is that she never suffered any memory loss and was totally alert until her last three days. She was able to go for a ride with me just one week before she died in her sleep. How wonderful was her life and death.

My parents never bought a new car until they were in their late 50s. We had a 1939 Chevy until 1957! Then they bought a used 1954 Chevy. Then finally they bought a new 1963 Chevy. My dad insisted that I be an attentive driver, as I would be driving this car during my college years. He thought I would be a better driver if the car did not have a radio. Yes, at that time a radio was an option in a new car. A friend of mine at the time famously said (not in reference to my dad's decision), "A car without a radio is like a home without a toilet." I never told my dad that quote.

I also remember my idol, Milwaukee Braves third baseman Eddie Mathews. I felt connected to Eddie because he drove a 1957 powder blue Chevy convertible. Wow! I was 13 and this was frosting on the cake. As an aside, this also says a lot about how much larger major league salaries are today. Can you imagine a star today driving a Chevrolet—his only car? Professional sports have changed a great deal since then, and so, too, has the auto industry. ∎

3

The Golden Age of the Auto Industry and Why It Ended

From the end of WWII until the 1980s, Janesville and much of auto manufacturing in America experienced a golden age of good-paying, middle-income jobs with excellent benefits available to a workforce that could get hired with few previous skills. The strong history of the General Motors plant in Janesville since opening in 1923 led us to believe and hope that it and all the jobs would be here to stay. This feeling was strongest in the golden age. Life was great and looked even greater in the rearview mirror.

Millions of jobs were in plants with unions. Unions, I believe, have done much to improve the lives of American families.

Unions fought for the eight-hour day and getting rid of the seven-day work week. They sought better working conditions and protection against unfair treatment by management. Unions bargained for benefits, health insurance, pensions, and wages in a way an individual employee couldn't.

However, I do think it is important to acknowledge that during the so-called golden age, unions had a lot of help that many have not acknowledged when evaluating this period. It's something unions and workers, whether in a union or not, do not have now.

What were the basic economic facts of life during this golden age that have changed, and where did the help come from? Consider that from the '40s until the '80s:

• The big three auto manufacturers were General Motors, Ford, and Chrysler, plus a fourth, American Motors. Foreign competition, particularly from Japan, had not yet pierced the domination of the big three.

• Fuel efficiency was not an environmental or economic issue, and gas prices were low for most of that era. I remember gas was 25 cents a gallon in 1963. People could afford the larger, less fuel-efficient American vehicles, and many Americans loved them.

• Workers at the big three (and American Motors) were all members of one union: The United Auto Workers (UAW). Put simply, if the union bargained for a 5 percent pay raise and better benefits with one company (they always had a "target" company that they bargained with first), all other auto companies could afford to agree to them, too, because costs would go up for all, and they could just raise vehicle prices. There was no foreign competition to hamper this. Americans just kept buying American-made vehicles.

So, what blew up this world? I see three significant factors:

1. New technology. Inventions have forever affected the workplace, but most of the inventions and technological advances did not generally replace the worker. The computer and the robot changed that. The Janesville plant's workforce peaked at 7,100 in the early 1970s. By early 2008 that number had dropped to 3,500. This reduction was due almost entirely to technology/robots and other efficiencies, not to work being taken out of the country.

2. Globalization. The United States became part of a worldwide economy, no longer the mostly closed economy of the golden age. U.S. manufacturers moved production and therefore jobs to other countries where they could pay wages and benefits at a fraction of their costs in the U.S. Globalization significantly reversed the leverage of the unions. Companies could essentially say, "Settle for less or we will take the jobs overseas." This new reality eventually led the UAW to agree in the summer of 2008 to a two-tiered wage system. All current employees would stay at their present levels, but new employees would be paid considerably less. At GM the new wage was $14.85 per hour. To put this in context, consider that the basic pay for assembly line workers in Janesville in 2008 was $28 per hour! These numbers did not include the additional costs of benefits. The UAW would only have agreed to this if they had no other choice. Globalization had taken away much of the UAW's leverage.

3. Gas prices. The big three made a general decision to concentrate on the more profitable larger vehicles and fell behind the curve on the smaller but more fuel-efficient vehicles (Honda, Toyota). In his 2010 auto industry book, *Overhaul*, Steven Rattner offers a new explanation for why General Motors

did not develop fuel-efficient vehicles to compete with the latest Japanese vehicles. It wasn't that GM was blind to the increasing popularity of the more fuel-efficient vehicles, especially as gas prices began to rise. The problem was that GM could not produce a car at the competitive price of $20,000 and make a profit. So they just said no. They were unwilling to make the difficult decisions necessary to reduce the costs associated with their large number of models, their agreements with dealers and suppliers, and their employee payroll. So the protections of the golden age were gone.

Even during the golden age, however, the UAW still had to bargain hard for better contracts, and this frequently meant going on strike to help them succeed at the bargaining table. But as the 1980s dawned and the sun set on the golden age, it was clear the world had changed. One need look no further than the GM plant in Janesville. ıl

4

1984-1986: Silence from Detroit

The more I studied the relationship between the Janesville plant and the General Motors Corporation, the clearer it became that GM's commitment to the Janesville's plant was more fragile and at more potential risk than most people in Janesville realized, or at least wanted to acknowledge.

I believe the events of three years—1984 to 1986—reveal the most about the real GM relationship with Janesville and its plant. There are other indicators and events that I discuss in this narrative, but as I look back at the long relationship that began in 1923 and ended in 2008, it is best understood by a close look at those three years.

In 1984, GM announced it would move the full-sized pickup called the CK, included in the GM Sierra and Chevrolet Silverado production in Janesville, to the new GM plant in Fort

Wayne, Indiana, in 1986. The move would cost the Janesville plant about one-half of its workload and over 1,800 jobs.

Janesville workers were offered the opportunity to take jobs in Fort Wayne. If they stayed in Wisconsin, they could only hope that GM would replace the lost full-sized pickup truck with a new product at the Janesville plant. This announcement mobilized me and many others to try and get GM to change its mind and keep the CK in Janesville. Also, during 1984, 1985, and 1986, GM announced no plans to put a new product in Janesville. This was the view from Janesville. GM Detroit explained that there was no product to move to Janesville during that period.

When there was no signal from Detroit about assigning a new product to Janesville, that was actually a very strong signal. "We don't care if we give you any new product," is how I would interpret it. "Our CEO doesn't care if we close your plant. You are going to be the half empty, two-story, outdated, oldest plant we own."

In 1985, Janesville plant manager, Mike Cubbin, asked to have the state build a new interchange on Interstate 90. The highway was right next to Janesville and actually went through part of Janesville. I-90 was the main route for bringing truckloads of parts for assembling the vehicles at the plant. Without a new interchange, trucks needed to drive through several city streets to get to the plant. The interchange cost Wisconsin taxpayers $7 million.

I was state Senate majority leader at that time and anxious to accommodate GM's needs. We passed a bill with the total support of Governor Anthony Earl, and the new interchange, referred to as the Avalon Road Interchange, was completed in the late 1980s. Despite the approval of this new interchange, GM would not make any guarantees regarding the future of the plant and remained silent about any replacement product.

This was a typical example of the power relationship between GM and Janesville, its elected officials, and Wisconsin state government. GM held the power and we always tried to meet their needs. But they held all the cards.

Governor Anthony Earl

In 1986, the workers at GM faced some difficult choices: (1) take a job in Fort Wayne 270 miles away from Janesville and either move there with the potential family disruption or commute, allowing family to stay in Janesville, (2) face a layoff in Janesville and gamble on GM giving Janesville a replacement product, or (3) if you had 30 years of service (which included workers as young as 48) take retirement with a buyout. These were life-changing decisions that I doubt GM management in Detroit bothered to consider.

About 1,200 workers went to Fort Wayne. Another 500 were laid off, and the rest retired. Thousands of workers, spouses, and their children faced a new and uncertain future. The north side of the Janesville plant went silent in 1986—over a third of the plant.

Let me now state the obvious. GM had the taxpayers agree to pay for a new interchange ($7 million) in 1985 and emptied over a third of the plant the following year. Gratitude is not the first word that comes to my mind. As the legislator who authored the bill to provide the money for the interchange, I was not personally hurt financially, nor my family disrupted, but I felt powerless.

The full-sized pickup departure to Fort Wayne meant that all that was left in the plant was the Chevrolet Cavalier and the Cadillac Cimarron. This was better than nothing, and it kept

DISASSEMBLED

the plant open. However, the Cavalier and Cimarron were not exactly vehicles you wanted to bet the future on. It was critical to convince Detroit to assign another vehicle to be assembled in Janesville.

With the plant one-third empty, the Janesville GM situation in the mid-1980s was a serious one, and GM in Detroit remained silent on any plans to send a new product to Janesville when one became available.

Wisconsin Congressman Les Aspin was pushing Detroit from Washington to give Janesville a new product, and GM could not ignore Aspin, the chairman of the House Armed Services Committee, because GM had defense contracts.

Janesville had that going for it, as well as an alignment of convenience between GM Janesville management and the UAW Local. One needs to distinguish between the local GM management in Janesville and company headquarters in Detroit. There were two GM managements.

I don't mean to say that GM management had two different management structures. All GM management, of course, reports in one structure that leads to the board and CEO. As a practical matter, though, there were differences in GM management interests depending on whether you worked in top GM management in Detroit or local GM management in Janesville or other plants around America.

The final decision-makers on the Janesville plant's existence, whether it stayed open or closed, whether the products it assembled expanded or contracted, were in Detroit, not in Janesville nor any other city with a plant. If Detroit management did come to Janesville, it was to meet with the local management staff and then leave town. It would be the rarest of circumstances for them to have had any relationship with the community: the city leadership, the media, the chamber of commerce, or any community group. They had no emotional ties to Janesville and could make a case that big decisions must be made in the overall interests of the corporation, not based on personal feelings toward any particular plant.

These were, however, human beings, and it is impossible to conclude that they had no personal feelings. This reality gave some tilt to the plants closest to where top management lived in Michigan, to the plants closest to Detroit, and possibly to plants where executives worked on their way up the corporate ladder.

The other group of GM management was working in Janesville, and most would stay in Janesville over their careers. Many grew up in Janesville and wanted the plant to remain open for a long time. The plant manager and a few others in top management were likely on a career path where Janesville was a stop for a few years before moving up the corporate ladder. This is typical of most large corporations. However, they relied on the local foremen, general foreman, shift superintendents, and superintendents of the body shop, trim shop, paint shop, and chassis. There was also front office management of payroll, human resources, etc.

The personal interests of this large, local GM management team became more closely aligned with the interests of the workers in the UAW during hard times, including threats to the future of the plant.

A general observation of human nature is that people who do not agree with each other but find themselves in a rowboat in the middle of the ocean, realize that they all need to row in the same direction.

The two most likely scenarios were that it would be closed completely or get a new product to utilize the whole plant. It did not seem likely that GM would leave it half empty for an extended period.

The impending loss of jobs on both the management and union side, and the very uncertain future, led both groups to try and agree on changes in plant operations to impress Detroit and hopefully lead to a new product in Janesville. They were all in the same boat. Closing the plant would have meant the elimination of nearly 2,000 more UAW jobs and over 150 management and non-union jobs. Also, over 1,500 jobs at area supplier companies would be lost.

The response in Janesville by management and the UAW was impressive. The goal was to improve quality and efficiency to secure long-term job security in Janesville.

So what did Janesville management and Local 95 do?

The great news for Janesville was that we had two key people in the principal jobs on the management and union side. They got together in 1986 to figure out how to get Detroit's attention, and they had a powerful supporter in Washington, D.C.

Their action and the support of the UAW made all the difference in GM's immediate future in Janesville. Les Aspin then played a crucial role in getting Detroit to assign a new product to Janesville. It was a massive effort involving Les, Janesville GM management, and UAW Local 95, and it is worth a closer look.

The first step taken in early 1986 was when Janesville management and UAW 95 jointly hired Jim Harbour and Associates to study and recommend necessary changes to survive in the American auto and truck industry. This was a remarkably good sign that management and labor could agree on who to hire to help them and to jointly pay the costs.

Who was Jim Harbour? He had been a longtime Chrysler executive who left to start Harbour and Associates. He made a name for himself by uncovering waste and inefficiency in the big three auto company factories. He was sometimes a pain in the side of many U.S. auto executives, but the annual Harbour

Report became an industry bible. It inspired the big three to improve productivity to match their Japanese rivals. Harbour was on the cutting edge of what is called the Lean Manufacturing Movement.

The Harbour Report's most compelling finding was the estimates of the productivity of American versus Japanese car companies. They assigned the differences to management and operating practices. The trends were tracked on an annual basis. Harbour's core emphasis was on lean thinking. By the time they were hired in Janesville, Harbour had become a highly respected, impartial industry analyst.

The choices for the Janesville plant and its employees were to keep doing things the same way or make changes to be competitive going forward and impress Detroit. Their choice can be seen in the following timeline detailing the key actions taken to make Janesville an attractive place to assemble a new product.

A special meeting took place in Janesville on February 21, 1986, between Buick, Oldsmobile, Cadillac, and the truck and bus division to discuss possible uses for the truck side of the plant after that product was transferred to Fort Wayne.

Late in February, Jim Harbour made a presentation to management and union representatives with the aid of two, one-hour videos addressing changes necessary to compete and survive in today's market, including addressing the ever-increasing flood of imports. It was decided by management and union representatives to share this information in full with all salary and hourly employees through presentations known as the Harbour Tapes. This task was completed in April 1986.

Then on Saturday, July 26, a special meeting of the UAW was held to obtain permission from the membership for their union representatives to meet with management to investigate possible local agreement changes to help secure a new product for Janesville. Any proposed agreement changes would then have to be brought back to the membership for ratification. The membership granted this request.

Negotiations to make changes took place during the next seven weeks. All aspects of GM's operation were analyzed down to laundering coveralls, aprons, and work gloves. Many proposed changes addressed the fact that management and union members were all in the same boat, realizing that if Janesville did not have a product to build, all of the jobs would be lost. A brochure was distributed to all employees in September 1986 with the proposed changes. Subsequent meetings were held throughout the facility by union representatives to answer questions. On Saturday, September 20, 1986, and the next day, special meetings were held to answer all questions and concerns and then vote on the proposed changes. The proposed changes were ratified by production workers, (basically assembly line workers, 76.1 percent) and skilled trades (54.6 percent).

The following are some of the changes and implementation dates:

- Open parking, 9/29/86: All parking became first come, first served. Reserved parking stalls for management were eliminated. This applied to all hourly and salaried employees, including the plant manager. Executives with company cars did have a separate area to park, but they were not near the front row.

- No punch out, 9/29/86: Hourly employees would no longer be required to punch out at the end of their shifts. This requirement led to long lines of employees waiting to leave the plant. I remember these frustrating lines from my time in the plant in the 1960s.

Note: These first two items were designed to show that Janesville was a team, and union members and local management were all in it together, rather than reflecting actual savings for the plant. Janesville was the only GM facility to do this.

- New rates and classification, 10/27/86: All production employees were increased to the inspection rate (a pay raise), and the number of job classifications was reduced from 90 to three. Janesville was the only plant to do this. This was a big deal to increase efficiency.

- Four day/10-hour work schedule and alternative work schedules, 12/86 (this was approved by 81 percent in a separate, second vote by UAW membership): This vastly improved efficiency by eliminating the previous overtime after 8 hours agreement. One example of tremendous cost savings was the huge ovens used in the paint department. Operating these ovens only four days per week compared to five days was a major efficiency improvement. Skilled trades went to straight 8-hour shifts with no lunch allowing 24-hour coverage, which eliminated one-half hour overlapping shifts having two employees on the same shift doing the same job. Skilled trades also went to a Sunday night start, allowing them to prepare for Monday morning production at straight time rather than double time as in the past. Janesville was the only plant to use these work schedules. This may have been the biggest change of all. Employees traded longer hours per day for working fewer days per week and a longer weekend. GM realized huge savings.

- All of the changes above were important. The two changes directly above, however, were a big deal at the time, and events of the coming years 1987 and 1989, and for nearly 20 more years after, would solidify their central importance to GM's continued presence in Janesville.

- Matrix inspection, 10/27/86: All production employees receiving the inspection rate (i.e., a high wage rate) would mark on a matrix inspection ticket any part of their work assignment they were not able to complete properly. This eliminated the need for an additional inspector doing the same work assignment. Who better to know, other than the employee, if something was missed or not completed properly in the first place? This caused a tremendous improvement in efficiency and a major improvement in quality. Janesville was the only GM plant to do this.

- Equal opportunity job selection (EOJS job posting), 10/27/86: With the reduction to three classifications and a new transfer agreement, this became the most efficient transfer agreement in GM and the only plant to do so.

- TYME machines, 10/30/86: TYME machines (ATMs) were placed in the main entrance/exit lobbies of the plant to make their use convenient for all employees.

- Eliminated skilled trade welders, 10/86: Welders were eliminated and allowed to transfer into a different trade with training provided. Trades that did not previously weld were trained to weld. This resulted in a decrease in manpower and an increase in efficiency. This change had been made in other GM plants.

- Suggestion coordinators added, 10/86: Two hourly and two salaried coordinators were added to investigate and expedite suggestion implementation under the Suggestion Program. Every suggestion implemented either improved quality, saved money, or more often, both. Janesville was the only location to implement this approach.

• 1987 Local contract agreement, settled 10/4/87: Language was added that would be implemented if Janesville received a second product to replace the truck line that moved to Fort Wayne.

How did the 1986 agreement get done? Big agreements need big leaders—at least one on each side. So it was with this agreement. Plant manager, Mike Cubbin, was the key management person. I got to know him in 1985 during the proposal to build the new I-90 interchange. I found him to be a good people person. He could work with almost anyone, and that certainly included the UAW. The key union person, without a doubt, was the shop chairman, Jim Lee. If he couldn't reach an agreement that made these changes *and* sell it to the membership, there would be no agreement.

This was not just another agreement. This was management and the union each giving on big issues that would have been highly unlikely in the 50 previous years. The first vote was far from unanimous. Seventy-one percent of assembly line workers and 56 percent of the skilled trade workers voted yes.

Many union members' historical opinion of the "white shirts" (management) was, to say the least, not positive or friendly. Many on the management side never liked the idea that unions shared power over how they ran the company. There were also many on both sides who respected each other.

The new agreement accomplished its purpose. It did indeed get Detroit's attention, and putting more workload in Janesville now made economic sense from GM's standpoint: more cost cutting, more efficiency, likely more profitability, and a message that labor relations were in good shape.

It also applied pressure on Detroit to put another product in Janesville for a less discussed reason. If after Local 95 agreed to all these changes and then Detroit gave them nothing, what message would that send to every other UAW Local? Well, those locals would say, "Why should we make concessions when we saw what happened to Janesville? They agreed to big changes and were given nothing in return."

Who was Jim Lee, and how did he get this done? He was a no-nonsense (on work issues) guy who had served in Vietnam, and he did not care about union politics even though the shop chairman was an elected position. A person worried about their election future in the union would not have stuck their neck out as far as Lee did.

Jim Lee

Jim Lee was observing the changes taking place across GM in 1986. He saw that plants in Norwood, Fremont, and Southgate had already closed. He saw increased use of robots, automotive technology, and paint shop technology changes, which were a specific worry for Janesville with its older paint shop on the second floor. This required lifts to get vehicles up to the second floor to paint and then take them back down for further assembly. Lifts cost money and can have mechanical issues. GM also had built elevators to move materials and equipment between floors. These costs did not exist at plants with just one level.

Jim Lee realized that Janesville needed to get ahead or they would fall behind.

The elected leader of the union is, of course, the president. He or she is the administrative leader and the public face of the union—an important position. But it is the shop chairman who negotiates contract changes with management and then must sell them to the membership. It helps, of course, to have the support of the president.

I believe changes within almost any sector of American life are safer to oppose than support in the beginning. The status quo is powerful, and the opponents of reform can predict all the terrible things that will happen, while the supporters cannot prove that the yet to be implemented changes will work or be beneficial.

Jim Lee faced all of this, but he knew that for the long-term existence of a plant in Janesville, it had to be done. He told friends that he could lose the shop chairmanship, and a few years later he did.

All the workers and all of Janesville and the surrounding communities can be grateful that Jim Lee was the shop chairman in 1986. He understood that a half-empty plant could easily become a completely empty plant. His great strength was that he was not afraid to fight the status quo, and he understood that sometimes compromise was necessary for the greater good of the union and the company. He got it done. The union voted to accept all the changes in the meeting in the fall of 1986.

Jim Lee is now deceased. I knew Jim fairly well and liked him a lot. He had this incredible way of speaking to make a point that sometimes dazzled everyone. My favorite story about Jim's skills and wordsmithing occurred in 1987. A Janesville management team and a UAW team were in Detroit to discuss their proposal to get the medium-duty truck to Janesville. The Janesville management/union proposal had been made. This was their final shot.

The meeting was about to end when Jim spoke up and told the Detroit group the following: He said he had served in Vietnam and would have given his life for the men he served with. He said he would do the same for the Janesville UAW workers. Then he said, "How long can a dog walk around in a cold barn with a frozen turd in his mouth?"

I believe Jim probably meant how long could Janesville survive with a half-empty plant after making historic changes in the 1986 agreement. Yet it had gone since 1984 with no word from Detroit on a replacement product. This makes the barn even colder and the taste in the mouth even worse.

The meeting then broke up, and the Detroit management team went to a different room to discuss the decision by themselves. While they waited, some of the Janesville folks wondered whether Lee's closing comments had helped or hurt the cause.

Later, when the Detroit team returned, their leader said of Lee's closing comments, "I have never been spoken to in a meeting like this in that manner, and I have never been more impressed." Sometimes at crucial times in politics, business, or life, a person emerges to save the day. In Janesville in 1986, it was Jim Lee.

My friend Stan Milam wrote a spot-on article for the *Janesville Gazette* about Jim Lee on February 15, 1989. Milam is the son of a UAW member. His father retired after over 30 years at the plant. Milam pointed out that unions used to "file grievances, set a strike deadline, strike, then settle and promise better working relationships. But the same process would start again." He also pointed out that the auto industry was caught in a volatile marketplace that changed a 50-year adversarial relationship with management.

Jim Lee got this. He seemed to embody the old saying: "He could see around the corner." Jim grasped the future. Leaders who understand this and act on the new realities need guts because change is hard for many in politics and unions. Their vision is eventually acknowledged and appreciated, but pushing for change can put you in a lonely place. There are always the second guessers, and in Lee's case, the rumblings that any change he agreed to was somehow selling out the union.

Lee said in the Milam story that he often felt like a "big fire hydrant" or like he was "following a manure spreader." He always had a great way with words. Jim Lee said he was proud of three things in his life: "Two wonderful kids—their mother did a great job. I got to serve my country [in Vietnam]. And I got to represent the people of the UAW Local 95." **ıl**

5

Walter Reuther, Organized Labor, and Social Change

I regard Jim Lee as a hero in this story. In my Janesville-GM research, I encountered a few other remarkable individuals, and though their connection to the 1984–2008 period was less direct than Jim's, I want to tell you about Walter Reuther, Doris Thom, and John Scott. Each played a significant role in transforming the UAW, specifically the Janesville plant, into a place where there were gender and race equality.

I will write about John Scott and the issue of race later in this narrative, but I wanted to mention him along with Reuther and Thom, whom I profile in this chapter and the next, for I regard all three as heroes. It was a pleasure learning and writing about all of them.

You really can't talk about or understand the UAW, and therefore Local 95 in Janesville, until you know Walter Reuther. This man survived an assassination attempt by someone with a double-barreled shotgun. This man walked the streets of America, including Selma, Alabama, in 1965 with Dr. Martin Luther King, Jr. for civil rights and was next to Dr. King when he gave his "I Have a Dream" speech at the Lincoln Memorial in 1963. He fought hard for increases in social security benefits for all Americans and was a leading advocate

Dr. Martin Luther King Jr with Walter Reuther

in the fledgling environmental movement in the 1960s until his death in 1970. He helped Jewish students hide from the Nazis in Germany in the 1930s.

People who do not know of Walter Reuther might assume from the above examples of his actions and causes that he was perhaps a United States senator with presidential ambitions. Walter Reuther never ran for public office. He was a longtime union activist and president of the UAW International Union from 1946 until 1970. Yes, the president of a labor union used his position to improve the lives of all Americans, not just the lives of his union members and their families. I consider Reuther one of the great American leaders of the 20th century—not just one of the great labor leaders.

Walter Philip Reuther was born in Wheeling, West Virginia, in 1907. His parents were socialists and pacifists of modest means. He had four brothers and one sister. Walter quit school at age 15 in 1923 to get a job to help support his family. (I might mention that my father quit school at the same age in the same year for the same reason. I am proud of this coincidence.)

Reuther later moved to Detroit where jobs were more plentiful than in West Virginia. He was hired by Ford Motor Company as a tool and die maker. While he worked nights at Ford from 1926 to 1933, he completed his high school education and three years of college. Ford fired him for engaging in "labor union activity" in the plant.

Walter Reuther

Reuther and his brothers then left the United States to see the world. It was 1933 and there were few jobs available during the Depression. It was on this trip that they lived in Hitler's Germany and helped the Jewish students escape the Nazis. This experience made a lifelong impression on Reuther and later led him to support President Franklin Roosevelt's view that America needed to enter World War II to stop Hitler.

The Reuthers also lived in Russia and worked at a Ford plant there. They saw what communism looked like under Joseph Stalin. This experience made Reuther a strong anti-communist for the rest of his life. This strong feeling would show itself when he was later elected president of the UAW.

Reuther and his brothers returned to America in late 1935. He had great difficulty getting hired as he was on a "black list." He was, however, given a membership in the UAW's Ternstedt Local 86 in Detroit in 1936. This would be the launching pad that would lead him to the union presidency 10 years later. Those years would see him climb the union's leadership ladder.

Walter also met May Wolf in 1936, and they fell in love. They married after a six-week courtship. May would be his rock of support for the rest of their lives.

Walter became president of UAW Local 174 in Detroit and led a sit-down strike against a Ford supplier plant. Reuther negotiated a settlement including, among other issues, a guarantee that women workers would receive equal pay for equal work. Before the sit-down strike, men earned 32.5 cents per hour, and women earned 22.5 cents per hour. The agreement Reuther negotiated that ended the sit-down strike included a pay level of 75 cents per hour for men and women.

He continued his belief in the need for a union at Ford and, along with other men, started handing out pro-union literature outside the plant. He and several others were beat up by Ford security agents. There are pictures of a bloodied young Walter Reuther. This occurred on May 26, 1937, at the "battle of the overpass." The UAW has an official remembrance of this event every May 26.

Reuther's rise to the top levels of the UAW was propelled by his post-WWII offer that he would settle for a one percent raise if GM would open their books and show that a bigger pay raise would force them to raise car prices. GM was outraged and refused. Reuther's position was that GM, with its big wartime profits, while wages were frozen for over three years, did not need to raise prices because of auto worker pay raises. He wanted pay raised and a freeze on GM auto prices. This proposal received widespread attention.

America's conversion from a wartime economy to a peacetime economy was not smooth, and I don't think it could have ever been smooth. The basics of the big three automakers' dollar position at the end of the war was very different from the position of the workers.

The companies realized big profits from the government as they stopped producing vehicles for people and converted their plants to wartime machines to produce the tanks, planes, jeeps, ammunition, and whatever else the military needed to win the war. The workers, on the other hand, had their wages frozen for three and a half years.

The 1946 UAW convention included the election to a new term for the president of the union. Reuther became a candidate, opposing the incumbent, R.J. Thomas. Thomas was sympathetic to the communists. It is difficult for many of us in 2019 to realize the threat and power of communist influence in the American labor movement and, in this case, the UAW in the post-war 1940s.

Reuther had many good feelings toward socialism, but he was staunchly anti-communist dating back to the early 1930s when he lived for a time in Joseph Stalin's Russia. The 1946 convention in Atlantic City saw over 8,000 delegates vote for president. It was close. Reuther won by just 124 votes.

Reuther spent the next two years cleaning communist influence out of the executive board as well as mob influence out of the union. It nearly cost him his life. Reuther was determined to run an ethical, clean union. One of the many ways he ensured this was not to have the union be the administrator of its pension fund. Too much money risked the abuse of it.

Reuther also understood that there was money in benefits. He did not want to bargain for too much of the available money in wages which could be spent and gone. He wanted members of the union to get some of that money put into pensions and health insurance.

Reuther survived an assassination attempt on April 20, 1948. He was standing at the refrigerator in the kitchen of his home in Detroit. May was saying something and he turned to listen to her. It was lucky he did. Just as he turned, a man with a double-barreled shotgun shot him through his window. The blast shattered his right arm, and one of the bullets pierced his back and exited out his stomach. Had he not turned around at the moment the shots were fired, his chest would have taken a direct hit and almost certainly killed him. Reuther underwent months of therapy with some recovery of functionality in his arm. His daughter Elisabeth tells the whole story in her book *Reuther: A Daughter Strikes.*

The shooter was never brought to justice. A man who was with the shooter was caught, told of being paid by the mob, but escaped to Canada and never stood trial. The story of the FBI's (read: Edgar J. Hoover) lack of cooperation deserves a full book of its own.

Thirteen months after the attempt on Walter's life, his brother Victor, incredibly, met a similar fate. Victor was sitting in his living room chair when a person with a double-barreled shotgun shot him through his home's front window. Victor was hit in the face, throat, and chest. He lost an eye but survived. The Reuthers believed this was a message to Walter that the mob was still around.

The lack of effort by the FBI and Hoover to investigate the attempted assassination of Walter in 1948 and his brother Victor in 1949 led the United States Senate to take the highly unusual step of passing a resolution that called on the Department of Justice to "make all law enforcement facilities of the Department of Justice be available immediately to investigate and cooperate with local authorities in apprehending the criminals who attempted the assassination of Victor A. Reuther and earlier of his brother Walter P. Reuther."

Think about it. The United States Senate felt compelled to pass a resolution directing the Department of Justice to take the investigation of the assassination attempts more seriously. Wow! You can find additional documentation about this story in the appendix of the book *The Brothers Reuther and the Story of the UAW/A Memoir*, by Victor Reuther.

J. Edgar Hoover had taken the position that he did not have the authority to investigate the attempts to kill the Reuther brothers. Gangland-style shootings with a double-barreled shotgun combined with Walter's efforts to throw mob influence out of the UAW (and communist influence) and Hoover couldn't find the authority to investigate? An astounding commentary on the FBI under J. Edgar Hoover!

Reuther would have major security for the rest of his life, much of it paid for by the UAW. Walter Reuther's security helped keep him alive. His bravery can be seen when, despite all this concern, he marched down the streets of America with Dr. King, leaving Reuther exposed should anyone along the routes take a shot at him.

Reuther had been committed to running a clean union at the UAW and had succeeded, but he realized corruption anywhere in labor unions hurt everyone in the movement. Reuther made comments aimed at Dave Beck, the head of the Teamsters, and that union which had been in the headlines—stories exposing corruption and racketeering in its leadership. Reuther was also applying his comments to any other corrupt union that had not yet been exposed.

The following quotes are from Reuther's speech at the April 1957 UAW Constitutional Convention:

> I think that we can all agree that the overwhelming majority of the leadership of the American labor movement is composed of decent, honest, dedicated people....But, unfortunately, in certain unions the gangsters and the crooks and the racketeers have moved into positions of power.

We happen to believe that leadership in the American labor movement is a sacred trust. We happen to believe that this is no place for people who want to use the labor movement to make a fast buck. We say to these people, "If you want to make a fast buck, that may be your business, but you better make it outside of the American labor movement, because we are not going to tolerate gangsters and racketeers inside the American labor movement.

We say there should be no room for either crooks or Communists in the leadership of our kind of free labor movement.

American labor had better roll up its sleeves, it had better get the stiffest broom and brush it can find, and the strongest soap and disinfectant, and it had better take on the job of cleaning its own house from top to bottom and drive out every crook and gangster and racketeer we find, because if we don't clean our own house, then the reactionaries will clean it for us. But they won't use a broom, they'll use an ax, and they'll try to destroy the labor movement in the process.

We urge the McClellan Committee to expose every crook and every racketeer that they can find in the American labor movement, but we also insist that they expose with equal vigor, corrupt and crooked employers in America. All the corruption is not on labor's side.

These reactionary, corrupt managements would rather pay a bribe to a crooked labor leader than to pay a living wage to the workers represented by that crooked labor leader.

I say to the McClellan Committee, we will give you full support and cooperation. Go after the crooks in the labor movement, but go after the crooks in management's side of the problem, and when you find a crooked labor leader who took a bribe from a crooked employer, put them both in jail for about fifteen years and give them plenty of time to talk it over between themselves.

Maybe the briefest and clearest expression of Reuther's basic philosophy were the words he spoke in 1946 in his speech following his first election as UAW president:

"I view the labor movement as an instrument for social change, a vehicle with which we can improve the quality of the whole society." This was a broader view of a labor leader's job than most other labor leaders expressed. His actions and priorities remained consistent with these words for the rest of his life.

A man in the public arena as Reuther was from his first election until his death in 1970 gave many speeches and interviews. I believe listing some of his most memorable quotes will, in a relatively brief way, tell you much about this man:

There is no greater calling than to serve your fellow man. There is no greater contribution than to help the weak. There is no greater satisfaction than to have done it well.
—date unknown

Labor is not fighting for a larger slice of the national pie... labor is fighting for a larger pie.
—The New Republic, 1946

Civil rights and human freedom are indivisible. You cannot have those things unto yourself. You can be free only as your neighbor is free. —NAACP Convention, June 26, 1957

If you are not big enough to lose, you are not big enough to win.
—date unknown

Management has no divine rights. Management has only functions, which it performs well or poorly.
—1948

This union is not about Solidarity House [the UAW headquarters in Detroit], it is not about your local union headquarters: this union is about the men and women that we represent, and behind them their families.
　　—a firm message sent to his own leadership in April 1970

Labor has to make progress with the community, and not at the expense of the community. We are not fighting for more dollars—we are fighting for more purchasing power. If we get a wage increase and it is taken away with higher prices, we have made no progress.
　　—1948 debate with Ohio Senator Robert A. Taft

I love the following exchange between Henry Ford II, the head of Ford Motor Company, and Reuther while they were touring a Ford plant in the 1950s. On their tour they were looking at some robots (yes, robots in the 1950s) and Ford said, "Walter, how are you going to get that robot to pay your union dues?" Reuther responded, "Henry, how are you going to get that robot to buy one of your cars?"
　　—reported in a UAW-CIO conference report, January 1955

There is a direct relationship between the ballot box and the bread box. What we win at the bargaining table can be taken away in the legislative halls. The surest way to guarantee that your ice box will be filled with good food is to see that the ballot box is filled with good votes.
　　—UAW Convention, 1947

Well, I'm not sure what Reutherism is, but I can tell you what I believe. I believe, to begin with, that free labor and free management have a great deal more in common than they have in conflict.
　　—June 1946

(The above quote is exactly what the UAW and Janesville GM management figured out in the previous chapter.)

　　　　　　　　　　　　　　　　　　DISASSEMBLED

The struggle between freedom and tyranny is not an old-fashioned struggle for geography. This is a struggle for the hearts and minds of people.
　　—NAACP Convention, 1957

Education is the golden key that unlocks the potential of human growth.
　　—date unknown

We won the war. The task now is to win the peace. Let us go home motivated by the same spirit that motivated us back in 1936 and 1937 when all you could get for belonging to a union was a cracked head.
　　—accepting the UAW presidency in 1946

There was one more quote from well-known newspaper columnist Murray Kempton that I think grasps what a visionary he was. Kempton once called Reuther "the only man I have met who could reminisce about the future." The following story is, to me, the classic example of how Reuther's eye was always on all Americans and not just his union members:

While Reuther was negotiating pension increases for his retired members, he made an offer to management. If Social Security benefits were increased, he would accept lower pension increases for his members. An example would be if the UAW negotiated a 4 percent increase in pension benefits, but then Social Security benefits were increased by the equivalent of 2 percent, the UAW would accept just a 2 percent increase as his members would still get the originally negotiated 4 percent total.

Reuther's strategy was that this agreement would lead to the big three automakers going to Washington with their lobbyists to lobby for Social Security increases because an increase in Social Security benefits would reduce their pension increase costs for UAW members. Reuther had figured out a way to get

Social Security increases for millions of Americans who were not in the UAW, and for many, Social Security was their only income. Reuther was a major player in Democratic politics. He was, after all, the leader of a 1.5 million-member union.

There was a large field of qualified Democrats, mostly United States senators, seeking the Democratic nomination for president in 1960. Vice President Richard Nixon was almost a sure thing to be the Republican nominee. There were at least two Democratic candidates including Senator Hubert Humphrey of Minnesota and Senator Stuart Symington of Missouri, who had great voting records on labor issues. But Reuther decided to support Senator John F. Kennedy of Massachusetts. In the biography of her father, *Reuther: A Daughter Strikes*, Reuther's daughter said that her father preferred Kennedy because he had a decent labor record but was also young, vital, and had great personal appeal.

After Kennedy won the nomination, he invited Reuther to his home in Hyannis Port, Massachusetts, to meet with him and asked him to prepare a ten-page report on what Reuther thought were the most important programs for the betterment of America. His list included civil rights, health care, unemployment benefits, and a program that came to be known as the Peace Corps. This was vintage Reuther. He always had a world view beyond the narrower interests of his union members.

Reuther sometimes traveled with Kennedy on the campaign. Kennedy, of course, won a narrow victory, and Reuther was a valued ally and advisor to the president.

March 7, 1965, at Edmund Pettus Bridge in Selma, Alabama, is now known as Bloody Sunday. What was to be a 50-mile march for voting rights to the state capitol in Montgomery ended at the end of the bridge. The local law enforcement beat up the marchers, which led to the hospitalization of 50 people. Current Georgia congressman John Lewis was one of the marchers who was beaten.

Two days later, on March 9, 1965, another march was scheduled. At Dr. King's request, Reuther joined him in the march. This time President Lyndon Johnson sent federal troops to protect the marchers, and national TV coverage helped keep the 50-mile march peaceful. I went to Selma in 2015 and walked the same route over the bridge. What a moving experience that was for me.

Reuther died in April 1970. Walter and May were organizing a world environmental seminar at the UAW Family Education Center at Black Lake in Northern Michigan. Individuals from 17 nations were going to gather that summer to discuss how to protect the environment.

The Reuthers were flying up to Black Lake to check on the conference planning. I think it is incredible that an American labor leader was doing this. However, it was not surprising that Walter Reuther was doing this. It was consistent with his world view on issues that affect everyone, including his union brothers and sisters.

The weather was cloudy and foggy that day. The plane was within a mile of the airport when it crashed, killing all six passengers on board. His death was a worldwide tragedy, but what he was doing when he died was a surprise to no one who knew him. His funeral with May, his friend and the love of his life, was attended by a considerable number of major American leaders of that time.

Walter Reuther was gone, but what he stood for continued to affect America. His view of the role of the UAW for its members and the world would be continued by successors to come. He had the most foresight of any American labor leader of the century.

According to Victor Reuther in his book, *The Brothers Reuther*, Walter's last official act as UAW president in April 1970 was "the sharp and bitter telegram denouncing [President] Nixon for the waste of lives and resources in Indochina that were needed at home to fight poverty, renew our cities, build hospitals and schools, and make life more meaningful for our people."

It fits that Walter Reuther's last official act was not just about his union, but instead was about making life better for all Americans. He was also expressing his strongly held views against the divisive issue of that time: the war in Vietnam and the rest of Southeast Asia.

Among the UAW and Walter's great innovations was the creation of Supplemental Unemployment Benefits (SUB pay). In *The New York Times*, April 10, 1975, William Safire praised it as "Detroit's better idea." Safire wrote:

> This was an indirect approach to Mr. Reuther's dream of a "guaranteed annual wage" in an industry notorious for boom-and-bust production...
>
> SUB's shock absorber, like state unemployment insurance, is not welfare; it is essentially insurance paid for by the worker, as about 10 cents an hour of fringe benefit is set aside in a fund for lay-off emergencies. It was designed for the auto industry's fluctuation, not an extended recession, which is why funds are now running out...
>
> Of course Detroit's SUB funds are depleted. But having proved their worth in transforming what surely would have been hard times into what amounted to an income for unemployed auto workers with seniority, SUB funds will be replenished at a faster rate than before when the economy picks up...

And other workers—particularly those in the vulnerable building trades—will wake up to the need for putting something aside for a rainy season...

The example of SUB is trying to teach us something. Perhaps we have been listening too raptly to the theories of Lord Keynes and underestimating the practical genius of Walter Reuther.

What Safire doesn't clearly explain is that laid-off workers would receive their unemployment checks plus SUB pay, so the total came closer to what they were earning before they were laid off.

This book's appendix includes the titles of three books about Reuther. The UAW in Janesville has kept Walter Reuther's name and legacy alive. As noted earlier, the UAW Local 95 hall was named for Walter P. Reuther. Also, the new road built in 1990 to connect the Interstate interchange with the plant was named Reuther Way.

Perhaps more important than remembering Reuther is that Local 95 (much more so when the plant was open and there were thousands of workers in the plant and at the supplier plants) followed his direction of helping people with no direct connection to the plant. Their charitable giving on a range of causes is well known in Janesville and Rock County. They were contributors to the United Way and began the Christmas food drive called Bags of Hope that is now run by the Janesville School District.

Additionally, there have been no scandals in Local 95—something else that Reuther demanded of the UAW. Forty-nine years after his death, Walter would be proud of UAW Local 95.

The list of Walter Reuther's accomplishments is long, and the record indisputable proving how he used that position of power to impact his union and labor's growth, spur economic progress, help advance civil rights and anti-communist efforts within the UAW, advocate for environmental issues, gain influence in the Democratic Party, and become a key advisor to Presidents Kennedy and Johnson, to name a few. He drew much support along the way.

There is, however, another way for a person to exercise power to make change. I would call it the power of one. The story of Doris Thom, an employee at the Janesville GM plant, is a story of that kind of power. ⅼⅼ

6

Doris Thom and the Power of One

Before being hired at GM, Doris Thom had worked at several manufacturing plants in Janesville, going back to World War II, when she was one of so many women who went to work in plants and factories producing weapons for the war. Doris was a "Rosie the Riveter."

While working at Gilman Engineering in 1944, Doris experienced a rude introduction to the gender inequality of that era. She became pregnant with her and her husband's second child, and she was fired as her penalty for being pregnant.

Doris Thom
Photo credit Janesville Gazette

Those were the rules, and Doris left. Apparently you could not help win World War II if you were pregnant. Gilman had a union, too.

Doris described her departure in kinder terms than "being fired" in notes she wrote in 1997 and 2014 that were provided to me by her daughter, Pat. Doris wrote, "As was the case for all women at that time, I was expected to resign with no job waiting for me after the baby was born. That was the end of my time at Gilman."

Doris moved on and while still pregnant was hired as a cook at the German POW camp on the south side of Janesville. It appears you could cook for the German prisoners while pregnant, but you could not be a "Rosie the Riveter" to help us win the war.

Doris spent the next 10 years having a third child, raising a family, and, as she put it, "doing odd jobs and seasonal work." She worked for a while at the VFW Club as a waitress, but Doris said, "I got fired for slapping a diner who sexually harassed me." This was long before the "Me Too" movement!

By 1955, with her youngest child four years old, Doris heard that GM was hiring. She applied and was hired, even though she noted, "My oldest brother, Albert, who worked there and had been union president, was not encouraging and in fact tried to dissuade me from applying."

Doris started working at GM on April 5, 1955, and like almost all other female employees was assigned to work on the cushion line. The GM plant in that era was a male dominated building. All the company leadership and UAW leadership were men, much like society outside the plant and at other companies. By the early 1960s Doris was fighting for equality for women in the plant.

At that time the only other female workers at GM were the "candy wagon girls," who pushed a wagon of sweets and treats, and secretaries in the front office. About 80 women worked per shift on the cushion line. At that time, several thousand men worked on the large assembly lines such as the trim line, body shop line, paint shop line, the chassis line, and other functional areas. Doris eventually discovered that the women on the cushion line earned less per hour than the men did on the assembly lines.

I can attest to the physical difficulty of jobs on the assembly versus the cushion line after I worked on both the trim and cushion lines over the summers from 1962 to 1965. I was, as best I can recall, the only man on the cushion line. I was filling in for someone on vacation for a few weeks. There I was, a skinny 19-year-old with pimples, with 80 women. They all treated me very well. Maybe I seemed like a son to some of them based on our age difference.

Let me be clear. My trim line job and my cushion line job had almost the same degree of difficulty. There was no justifiable reason to have different pay levels. There were many tougher jobs in the body shop than mine on the trim line. Paying different wages based on the difficulty of the tasks would make some sense—but not based on gender.

Writing about Doris has caused me to ask myself a question I had not thought of in all the years since 1965. When I was moved to the cushion line, did I earn my original assembly line wage, or was it lowered to the cushion line wage the women were making? I have no way of getting an answer to that now, but I'd bet some money I kept getting my assembly line wage. I have no recollection of my paycheck being less. I was not aware then of the different levels of pay. I was just a kid getting good wages and waiting for the whistle to blow.

By 1965, Doris was active in the union and became the first committeewoman at the Janesville plant. While I was there in the early 1960s, I only ever heard the term committeeman. This was the person a worker could talk to regarding problems or issues with their job.

As Doris put it, "Upon my urging," she was sent to the Regional Women's Committee Meetings for the Regional UAW in Milwaukee. There was no women's committee in Janesville. Doris said, "I learned a lot. My eyes were slowing being opened." Doris learned in Milwaukee that women worked in many areas of other plants. So she asked herself, "Why couldn't I move from my job out into the assembly line jobs that paid more?"

Doris demanded that she be transferred to an assembly line job with the higher pay. She went to the office and applied for a transfer and was told no. The reason given was "past practice." To Doris, this phrase meant that she couldn't take a different job because no woman had ever done it before. She thought this sounded like "circular hogwash."

"I was starting to get mad," she noted, but then her Milwaukee friends told her about a newly passed federal law called the Civil Rights Act of 1964. It prevented employment discrimination based on factors such as "race and sex."

It is important to point out that Doris was challenging the pay disparity issue at the Janesville GM plant by herself with no public support. Her colleagues in Milwaukee were supportive, but she had no women's organization to help her with her fight and no activists to protest the situation on her behalf. She did not even have her union's support. She noted that "none of the women on the cushion line were allowed to go to any other parts of the plant, so I had no moral support. I was on my own." Women who are (still) fighting today for equality and exposing the serious issue of sexual harassment and equal pay for equal

DISASSEMBLED

work, both in the workplace and in general, are seeing support from other women and women's groups as well as many men, not to overlook growing legal support. Doris had no such help—only her determination to earn equal pay.

Doris, with the laws of our nation on her side, asked to meet with the plant manager and was granted a meeting. She again politely requested to be transferred to the assembly line at the pay level of the men on the assembly line. She made it clear she would pursue legal action if not granted this request. The plant manager granted her request.

Doris moved to the assembly line, but the beginning was not easy. Doris was assigned to one of the tougher jobs on the assembly line. Assembling an automobile requires that some work be done underneath the car. This work was performed while standing in a "pit" below the assembly line as the cars came down the line above the worker in the pit. This required the worker in the pit to continually work with their arms above their head. The workers in the pit had to lift a heavy air gun to attach weather stripping to the underside of car doors. Doris did this without complaint. Her daughter Pat told me of severe arthritis in her mom's shoulders later in life due to her work. Doris said men would make a pilgrimage to the pit to see "the woman." None of them ever talked to her directly. She said she felt like an animal in a zoo.

I can tell you from experience that there were hundreds of jobs that were physically less demanding than the job Doris was assigned. But Doris would not be defeated, and after a year her seniority qualified her for physically easier jobs, each job paying better than the last.

Sad to say, Doris received the silent treatment from all of the male workers around her. She described this in a talk she gave at the Janesville library in 2010. Doris endured this silent treatment without complaint. She said she eventually broke through their "wall of silence" by bringing in two cakes on her birthday and inviting them all to have a slice. After that they would say hi to her but nothing else for quite a while.

The issue of bathroom use soon surfaced. There were men's restrooms all over the assembly line area, but the closest women's restroom was about 200 yards from her work location. This resulted in Doris being gone from her job for longer than the allotted time during bathroom breaks. The time allotted was, of course, adequate for the men with nearby restrooms. Doris was talked to about this.

She offered a solution, asking to speak with her union representative and foreman. She told them that she could see a men's restroom from where she stood, and using that would eliminate the long time she was taking to get to the women's restroom. She said she would start using that men's restroom! Well, both men reacted the same way. They both said something like, "Doris, you wouldn't do that!"

Doris responded, "Just watch me!" Then Doris said, "I am a married woman and I have two sons. There is nothing that I have not seen." The two men saw they had a problem. Their solution was to allow more break time so that Doris could get to the women's restroom and back in time without difficulty.

At first, women on the cushion line were afraid to follow Doris's lead and ask to be moved to the higher paying assembly line jobs. Men were telling them that if they moved to jobs on the assembly line and couldn't do them, they would not be returned to the cushion line. They would instead be fired. This was all rumor, but when your job supports your family, you do not want to take chances and can be intimidated into staying someplace like the cushion line.

Doris wrote in 2014, "The relief men hated me, the fellows around me would not speak, and everyone greatly resented me. I would go home hurting from the job. My arms ached from lifting the gun over my head for hours on end. My husband, Hank, felt so bad and continually told me I didn't have to take this. He wanted me to quit. I said I'd rather die on that line before I would admit defeat."

Of Hank, Doris said, "He always encouraged me and supported my decision." She said it was not easy on her husband because he also worked at the plant and would get guff from fellow workers. "I guess you can't control your wife," was the common theme. Doris also said it wasn't easy on the rest of her family. Her children received calls telling them that their mother should get back on the cushion line.

Doris fought through many challenges in her first job on the assembly line, and within a few years the women on the cushion line started receiving equal pay with the assembly line workers. And women began to get hired to work on the assembly line.

I have told Doris's story. It does not speak at all well about the men on the assembly line that she encountered. It must be said that there were thousands of men on the assembly line that she did not come in contact with. Doris ran for office in the union. She became the first woman to serve on the union's executive committee and the first woman elected as recording secretary of Local 95. This means many men voted for her. She had earned their respect and confidence. Doris also played significant roles in organizations outside the plant. She was a founding member of the National Organization for Women (NOW). Wisconsin Governor Patrick J. Lucey appointed her in 1971 to the Governor's Commission on the Status of Women. She was one of the founders of Blackhawk Community Credit

Union, which began as a credit union for UAW members. She was president of the Rock County Democratic Women for 15 years.

Doris also received several state and national awards including the Janesville YWCA's Woman of Distinction Award, the United States Army-Navy "E" (for excellence) Award in April 1944, the Catherine Conroy Award (for women dedicated to the rights of women and labor) at the Wisconsin State AFL-CIO Women's Conference in 2001, and the Veteran Feminists of America honored her as an early Midwest feminist leader in 2004. But as Doris put it, "Awards and 'firsts' didn't matter much when I became pregnant with my second child."

Her daughter Pat told the Janesville Gazette that Doris was very active in an AIDS support group after one of her two sons died of the disease. Besides all the challenges and causes she fought for in the plant, in the union, and the community, she also lived with the greatest pain a parent can ever suffer—the death of their child. It says much about Doris that she dealt with this pain by working to help others affected by that disease.

Doris's father was killed in a work-related accident when she was young. All the railroad offered in compensation (this was before Wisconsin had a Workers Compensation Program) was a free railroad pass. Doris's mother refused to accept this and insisted that the railroad pay to support the family that lost a dad and husband. She won. Doris learned a lot from her mother.

Doris stayed engaged in UAW affairs until the end of her life. She was active on the UAW Women's Committee until 2017, the last year of her life. Doris said union activism unquestionably "increased her self-confidence and that as a white woman in a mostly (over 99 percent) white town, working with and befriending black people helped her to overcome her prejudices."

Her comment about her prejudices is remarkable from a woman who had faced so much prejudice in her own life because she happened to be a woman. This reflects the Janesville of her time and makes it so clear how far Janesville had to come. The city isn't perfect on this matter yet, but we get better with each generation.

Doris attended the Rock County Democratic Party annual dinner in May 2017. I had my last chance to shake her hand that night. My daughter Katharine was with me, and I made sure she met Doris, and they shook hands. Doris, at age 97, received a rousing standing ovation from the crowd of 300 that evening.

In a story written upon her death in November 2017, *Janesville Gazette* reporter Frank Schultz described Doris as "a working woman who broke down workplace barriers and became a Janesville community leader." Well said. I would add she became a UAW union leader and an activist at the state and national level.

In the 1998 book *Like Our Sisters Before Us: Women of Wisconsin Labor* by Jamakaya, Doris said, "I am very definitely a feminist. I've had to fight for nearly everything I've ever wanted. If you hadn't pushed back, you would have accepted what you were offered, and I wasn't willing to do that."

It took 20 years, the Civil Rights Act of 1964, and Doris Thom to break the glass ceiling at Janesville GM. This all raises an interesting question. If Doris had not been armed with the Civil Rights Act or if there had not been a Doris Thom, how many more years would it have been before a woman worked on the assembly line in Janesville? My guess is it would have been until Walter Reuther heard about it.

Doris Thom was the first woman to work on the assembly line at the plant. But did women ever work with men at the plant before that? The answer is yes, during World War II when the plant (and most plants beyond just auto plants) were converted to make the weapons and other items needed to fight the war.

The Janesville plant was converted in 1942 to make artillery shells. Between 1942 and August 1945 the plant produced 16 million artillery shells. Some of the employees were women— "Rosie the Riveters." Anna Marie Lux wrote a great story about this in the *Janesville Gazette* on August 22, 2015. This was the 70th anniversary of the end of war production.

The plant operated three shifts per day, seven days per week. Workers or their children told Lux that the workers did not tell people what they were making. They just said, "war production." They knew that old phrase "loose lips sink ships." One said, "We never knew who we might be talking to."

Other plants in Janesville also produced items to help fight the war. Parker Pen produced fuses. The Janesville Cotton Mill produced bandages, and Hough Shade made curtains to help dim lights during air raids. Lux's story made clear that all of those workers took their jobs very seriously, as they were doing them to help us win the war.

Women had largely not been in the factories of America prior to World War II. The war saw unknown numbers of women work in the factories building the weapons of war while millions of men were in uniform. It is quite interesting to me that after the war, Janesville GM (and I'm guessing other places in America) returned to the pre-war attitude of women not being allowed to work on the assembly lines. Doris Thom opened doors for women at GM in Janesville, but even after the signing of the Civil Rights Act in 1964 sexism persisted in many ways.

I interviewed a woman who worked at GM from the mid-1970s to the mid-1980s. She wished to remain anonymous but told me several stories about the harassment and insults she dealt with as one of the few women working on the truck line at that time. I could see these memories trigger strong emotions even 30 years later.

She recounted stories about being told she took a man's job away, about walking into the women's bathroom to find ketchup-covered condoms on the floor, and about finding pornographic images taped to the bottom of the cars when she worked in the pit.

When I asked her if she ever reported any of this to her union rep or foreman, she said she didn't think it would make a difference and might even make things worse. When talking with a sympathetic male coworker about these incidents, he advised her to "kill them with kindness." I would not be surprised if other women working at GM Janesville over the years had similar stories.

This chapter focuses on gender bias, pay inequality for women, and harassment of female workers at GM from the 1950s through the 1980s, but GM was not the only place this happened. There are other examples of gender inequality in the workplace from those years.

School boards would hire a man rather than a married woman, their logic being that the married woman had a husband to support her, so she didn't need the job as much as the man. So much for hiring the person who would be the best teacher! Just ask the next retired teacher over 70 years old that you talk to! I have a friend who told me his mom was a teacher and was married to his father. Her school board would have fired her (this was around 1940) had they known she was married. So his mom and dad lived about 40 miles away from her school district, and the school board never found out. They later moved to Janesville.

Sue Conley is a city councilwoman in Janesville. She retired from her job as executive director of the Community Foundation of Southern Wisconsin and prior to that was executive director of the YWCA of Rock County.

Sue told me the following about her experiences with sexism in the workplace in the 1980s. She posted for an internal promotion at the bank where she worked but was denied by the male bank president because " 'I was an attractive young woman who will probably get married and start a family soon.' Yes, he actually said those words," Sue said. Later, she was promoted by a different male bank president, but when she asked about the salary, she was told: "Because I didn't have a family to support, I would not receive the same pay as my male counterpart with a family." Sue said, "It was spoken with others in the room and accepted as the norm at that time."

All of these stories about behavior in the plant raise a question in my mind... was there a "typical" auto worker? There is no such category to put them in, even though I believe a lot of people have an opinion in their mind.

I make this conclusion from my own experience in the plant during four summers in the 1960's, and from discussing this with several retired auto workers with decades of time working in "the plant."

- There were employees without high school degrees and there were employees with college degrees. These college graduates worked there because it was the highest paying job they could find.

- There were very nice people and there were bullies.

- Some workers read the bible during breaks and some read pornographic magazines. Some read newspapers and Time magazine, and some read books.
- Some loved to talk and some hardly spoke at all.
- Some liked to play practical jokes and some didn't like them.
- Many were Democrats, but there was a minority who were Republicans. Some never expressed their political opinions at all.
- Many or most were generous with their time and money, willing to help out another worker who was having trouble of any kind or had lost a loved one. Workers would help cover for a sick coworker or even one who had had a little too much to drink.
- And on and on...

It is important to tell these stories and remember the women who endured the abuse and pushed for equality as we continue to fight for women's rights today. It is part of the larger Janesville-GM story, which by 1987, in the wake of the 1986 new labor agreement, was looking brighter. For those who cared, there were also storm clouds on the horizon. ▮▮

7

The '86 Contract: Positive Changes

I n 1987, GM announced that the Janesville plant would be awarded a medium-duty truck line. There had been ongoing disagreements at the Pontiac, Michigan, plant between the company and the UAW. The disputes were not resolved, and GM decided to move medium-duty truck production out of Pontiac. Where was there space available? Janesville competed with two other plants. We won!

The medium-duty truck production would start in 1989. Laid-off workers would return to work. New workers would be hired. But those 1,200 who went to Fort Wayne had to sign an agreement that they could not return to Janesville for at least two years if the plant were awarded a new product. The executives calling those shots on the 37th floor at corporate headquarters never had personal contact with the employees and their families affected by their decisions.

Janesville was closer to full strength again. Yet the behavior of GM between 1984 and 1986 tells all one needs to know about GM's true commitment to Janesville. Timing of the move to Fort Wayne and the labor dispute in Pontiac, along with the efforts of Les Aspin and the important 1986 agreement, worked to Janesville's advantage.

Huge praise was heaped on Local 95 and Janesville management in 1989 for reaching the 1986 agreement. Along with that praise came more great news for Janesville. GM announced on February 13, 1989, that they were awarding Janesville the production of the next generation of large SUVs, specifically Suburbans, Blazers, and Jimmys, starting with the '92 models. This occurred while President Mike O'Brien led Local 95. The new production would begin in 1991 with 3,300 workers on two shifts.

The contract changes agreed to by Local 95 and local management at the end of 1986 had resulted in two new product lines being awarded to Janesville. Medium-duty trucks were awarded in 1987. Jim Lee's great work was properly recognized after the two new products were assigned to Janesville. However, it is important to acknowledge the contribution of the two Local 95 presidents during the 1986–1989 period: John Dohner, Sr. and Michael O'Brien. These two presidents supported Jim Lee. This made Lee's efforts much easier. Making significant changes without the support of the presidents would have been more difficult.

Stan Milam noted in the article discussed earlier, and I agree, that Jim was able to keep the partially empty Janesville plant on GM's front burner with the contract changes he agreed to in 1986, and it paid off big time.

A respected independent auto analyst, Ronald Glantz, was quoted in the *Janesville Gazette* on February 16, 1989, giving credit to the 1986 changes.

"The big three have all awarded new production to plants—such as Janesville—with modern, innovative work agreements," Glantz said. "GM has closed newer plants and moved work to older plants that produced higher quality."

Again, praise to Jim Lee. The job of selling the new contract also fell to Lee. He succeeded, and with the 1989 SUV announcement, confirmed beyond any doubt that Jim Lee's vision, guts, and leadership in negotiating the 1986 contract were a game-changer for the Janesville plant for 20 years.

Glantz, the industry analyst, made an insightful observation about the 1986 contract change that reduced job classifications from ninety to three. After discussing some practical ways that fewer job classifications can help the management of the workforce, he said, "With fewer job classifications, you get a different kind of worker. If a person spends many years doing the same repetitive job, that gets very boring. Some people don't mind that.... The person who prefers few job classifications may not be any smarter, but is more curious, a person who is more willing to make suggestions."

The suggestions from Janesville workers in 1988, just two years into the new contract, saved the company $4.5 million, and the workers earned more than $400,000 for their ideas, according to a story in the *Gazette*. Glantz also said in that story that fewer job classifications mean "you don't need as many surplus workers to cover sickness or deer hunting or whatever. If quality and productivity are not competitive, the plant will be closed," Glantz said. Glantz then predicted that GM would close between two to four such plants in the next few years. Thanks are due again to Jim Lee's foresight and courage.

Glantz dropped another major bomb in the *Gazette* story. He said innovative contracts (like Janesville's) are the *second* most crucial step GM must take to regain its competitive edge. "First, is reducing the number of white-collar employees," Glantz said, explaining that GM's many levels of bureaucracy led to conservative decisions, higher costs, slower response to market demands, and delays in developing new products.

It is worth noting that in 2019, GM CEO Mary Barra was criticized for her announcement that GM would eliminate 8,000 white-collar jobs along with 7,000 union jobs.

You will read later in this narrative about GM going broke and the Obama administration forcing them through bankruptcy in 2009. The problems at GM associated with excessive bureaucracy were the very complaints that Steve Rattner's 2010 book, *Overhaul*, described as GM Detroit's problem that helped cause the company to go broke.

Glantz recognized the difficulty in 1989! Rattner's book makes clear that GM management was fighting those decades-long problems in Detroit into 2009. **ıl**

8

Roger Smith and Les Aspin

What then of GM leadership in Detroit? It's time to talk about Roger Smith, the chairman and CEO of General Motors from 1981 to 1990. The events and challenges the Janesville plant faced during those years were serious, and we could hardly have had less of a friend than Roger Smith.

The announcement of the move of the full-sized pickup and the 1,800 jobs associated with it to Fort Wayne in 1984 occurred during his watch. This move would occur in 1986 and leave the Janesville plant nearly half empty. No one I have talked with on the union side or local management believed that the plant would stay half empty for an extended period of time. One of two things would happen. Either a new product would bring the plant up to full or near full capacity, or the remaining products in half the plant would be moved somewhere else, and the plant would close.

Between 1984 and 1986, when Janesville was left to speculate about its future, the UAW and local management launched its massive effort to agree to changes in the plant's operation that would impress Detroit. This effort, plus major pressure by Congressman Les Aspin in Washington—whose role I will address in this chapter—was significant in winning a new product for Janesville in 1987. Several sources have confirmed to me that this decision, while approved by Smith, was not his personal preference.

Some quotes from a newspaper article published in 1989, the day we learned SUV production was coming to Janesville, tell better than I can the feeling of long-term job security this announcement brought.

Janesville Gazette reporter Marcia Nelesen wrote after talking to several workers, "For workers with the least seniority, the Suburban could mean job security for the rest of their lives."

She quoted a worker who had 13 years of seniority (30 years of seniority was the minimum requirement to be able to retire with a pension), after saying he felt more secure in his job, "It's not just us [with 13 years in] but guys with two and three years in who can retire from here now."

I use these quotes to convey the euphoria of that time, but also to accentuate the feelings of most of Janesville that we had GM for as far as the eye could see. The plant closed 17 years later. Those workers with two or three years never got their 30 years of service. The guy with 13 years just barely made it to 30 years. This was the up and down history of GM in Janesville since its beginning in 1923—great euphoria followed by sadness when there was bad news.

Back to Roger Smith and his indifference (at best) toward Janesville's plant. Three days after GM announced Janesville's new product (SUVs) in February 1989, Ted Bornstein, a key aide to Les Aspin, saw Smith at an event in Washington, D.C. Smith had some words for Bornstein regarding the effort to get the new product in Janesville.

Bornstein's clear recollection of their meeting was that Smith pointed his finger at him and said, "You can tell your g.d. boss [Aspin] that Janesville is safe." Bornstein said those words were spoken bluntly with no hint of humor.

Smith died in 2005, but I have reflected on the message he was sending. The only conclusion I can draw is that if Janesville was "safe" with the new products, then it was "unsafe," at risk of being closed if Roger Smith had his way. The GM plant closed in 2008, but we might have seen the plant close earlier had it not been for the efforts of UAW Local 95, local management, and Les Aspin.

Aspin, who represented Janesville and Rock County as part of the First District from 1971–1993, was the Janesville GM plant's big-time supporter, protector, and powerful friend in Washington. He was chairman of the House Armed Services Committee, and General Motors had many Defense Department contracts that they cared greatly about. Aspin was crucial in securing the medium-duty truck line in 1987 when a half-empty plant had the UAW and local management worried about the future of the plant. Aspin also played a key role in 1989 in getting GM to award the SUVs to Janesville.

Les Aspin
Photo credit
Janesville Gazette

Aspin had been elected eight times to Congress and was popular in the district. His rise to power in Washington was impressive. In 1985 he had leap-frogged over several more senior members of the House Armed Services Committee to be elected its chairman. He was 48 years old and a rising star. He was widely acknowledged as the best-informed Democrat in the House of Representatives on defense issues. Aspin had a strong relationship with the UAW in Kenosha, Wisconsin, which had a Chrysler plant, and in Janesville with its GM plant. But 1987 was a challenging year for Congressman Les Aspin in his First Congressional District.

In addition to the effort to get GM to assign a new product to the half-closed Janesville GM plant, Aspin and new Wisconsin governor Republican Tommy Thompson had both been assured that Chrysler would not close the Kenosha plant. Both Governor Thompson and then Aspin staffer Ted Bornstein confirmed this to me. But Chrysler announced in early 1987 that it intended to close the Kenosha plant. Aspin and Thompson would work hard to save the Jeep engine work in Kenosha, but both felt deceived by Chrysler. The Jeep engine is a small fraction of workload that was saved. Governor Thompson told me in a 2018 interview, "Chrysler double-crossed us."

Governor Tommy Thompson
Photo credit
Janesville Gazette

Aspin summoned Chrysler Chairman Lee Iacocca to a meeting that included Thompson. According to Bornstein, Iacocca was very unhappy about having to be there. Aspin arranged to have the meeting in the Armed Services Committee room to remind Iacocca what committee he chaired. Both Thompson and Bornstein told me that the governor, a Republican, and Aspin, a Democrat, worked extraordinarily well together.

I should disclose to readers who don't know that I served on Aspin's staff from 1971 to 1974, and we then became good friends until Les's death in 1995.

Les told me during his time as chairman that whenever GM officials came to see him about their Defense Department contracts, he always began the meeting by simply asking, "How are things going at the plant in Janesville?" There are no known documents to verify this, but I have little doubt that GM got his message.

I have talked with Aspin's Washington staff person, Bornstein, and John Rodgers, his staff person on this in Janesville about Aspin's efforts during 1986 and early 1987. They both said GM's status was the number one issue in the entire First District.

Aspin met with GM Chairman and CEO Roger Smith on several occasions, as well as with GM staff in Washington and Detroit. Roger Smith did not care if the Janesville plant closed, but the overwhelming combination of the Jim Lee-led changes in Janesville and Aspin's efforts in Washington made it difficult to intervene in his staff's decision to award the medium-duty truck production to Janesville in 1987.

Les Aspin certainly helped get the medium-duty truck, but the highly important effort in Janesville between local management and UAW Local 95 played an essential role in getting the new product in 1987.

I have spoken with Aspin's 1987 Washington staff and with key people at Local 95 in Janesville. Both agree that it was the combination of Local 95 in Janesville and Les Aspin in Washington that led to the victory.

Aspin remained in his powerful position as chairman of the House Armed Services Committee from 1985 until President-Elect Bill Clinton asked him to be his Secretary of Defense following the 1992 election. Aspin was a popular choice. His whole career pointed to this pinnacle of a job. For years before Clinton was elected, he would seek out Aspin to talk about and learn defense issues.

Most people expected that he would likely be a successful defense secretary while Clinton was president. Many of us in Janesville felt Aspin's ability to protect the GM plant was just as strong or stronger in his new position as it was when he was in Congress.

Aspin, as Secretary of Defense, had reached the peak of his political ambition. It was true that in the early 1970s, in his first few terms in Congress he had hoped to become governor of Wisconsin or a United States senator from Wisconsin. For several reasons neither of these opportunities worked out. The two Senate seats were held by popular Democrats, Bill Proxmire and Gaylord Nelson. Nelson did lose in 1980, and Aspin would not have had a chance to run for that seat until 1986. Proxmire would serve until 1988. Aspin had become chair of the Armed Services Committee in 1985, so his interest in the Senate had come and gone. His first real chance to run for governor was in 1982, but by then his eyes were on the chairmanship.

How all this turned out for Aspin confirms for me that luck and good timing have very much to do with who is elected to high office, and that political winds for or against a candidate's party on election day often determine their fate. I have observed over nearly 50 years of Wisconsin elections that luck plays a huge role in the outcome of elections.

It did not go well for Aspin, and for reasons known and likely unknown, President Clinton fired Aspin after only one year. Les was gone by January 1994. The shock of Aspin's firing was felt in many places, but maybe no more directly than in Janesville and Rock County. The GM plant had lost its guardian angel in Washington. Aspin lost all his power and influence. Vanished like the wind! Aspin's absence hurt in 1997 when GM announced their intention to move the medium-duty truck back to Michigan. Janesville had no Aspin to save them.

Aspin died unexpectedly in 1995 at age 56. I had the great privilege to be asked by his family to speak at his funeral. What a high honor that was. Les died from a major stroke. Many of us knew he had potentially serious heart issues.

My view and the view of many who were close to him was, as the saying goes, "he died of a broken heart." Aspin's goals in life were all about public service. He lived for public service, and he died without it. The abrupt end in 1995 was devastating. His desire to serve was brought home to me when I had dinner with him in Milwaukee in April 1995. He died one month later. He told me he intended to run for his old congressional seat in 1996. The desire to serve was still strong.

The GM plant also needed a Les Aspin in 2008. A Janesville native, Paul Ryan represented Janesville in 2008. People know that Ryan rose to be Speaker of the House by 2015. This gave him real power. But we are talking about 2008, and he was then a young congressman with little seniority, and in the minority party.

GM didn't plan it that way, of course, but the company was lucky that in 2008 they needed not fear a politically powerful congressman or senator, should they choose to close the Janesville plant. If Ryan had been the speaker in 2008, I highly doubt GM would have closed Janesville that year. A year later, perhaps. In 2009, GM went through bankruptcy and closed twelve more plants.

That lay ahead—it seemed the distant future- as the '90s dawned, a mostly positive decade for the Janesville plant. ▮▮

9
The '90s and Early 2000s: Success and Controversy

After surviving the uncertainty of the '80s, the beginning of the 1990s was an upbeat time in the up and down life of a community heavily dependent on the auto and truck industry.

The medium-duty truck had been awarded in 1987 with production beginning in 1989, and the next generation of GM's SUVs had been awarded in 1989 with production beginning in 1991. Detroit had also recognized Janesville for their good labor-management relations. Producing a high-selling, high-profit vehicle was frosting on the cake.

GM had a planning process in which products would be awarded to plants for roughly seven-year blocks of time. It provided some certainty for everyone and allowed GM to recover the costs of changes made in a plant to produce that product.

The SUVs were extended in Janesville until 2005 and then again later until 2012. The history of GM in Janesville, and for most truck and auto companies, had frequently been affected by recessions, a depression, World War II, management-labor relations, and the politics in GM, in the UAW, and in Congress and the White House. History told us, "Never get too content." Still, with the extensions announced for a product in Janesville until 2012, the community felt reassured.

For the most part, the Janesville plant steamrolled its way through the 1990s thanks in large part to the groundwork laid in 1986 and the rest of the 1980s.

But controversial happenings in the plant and a subsequent GM decision to move the medium-duty line to Flint, Michigan, caused many to believe the events were related. It appeared to be a blunt message to Janesville and Local 95. The controversies involved gambling in the plant (parlay cards), drug selling outside the plant, and a tear gas incident.

The tear gas incident occurred on a hot summer day in the 1970s with the temperature outside above 80. The second shift had just started when two employees, Bruce Penney and Jim Conley, noticed a lot of smoke near the back of the plant. A tear gas canister caused it. This was serious, and the line was shut down, and workers in that area were directed to go outside.

A decision was then made to open the doors in that area of the plant in hopes of getting the smoke out of the plant. The reverse happened. The wind blew into the plant and spread the smoke over much more of the plant, and it was then evacuated.

What do you think many employees did while waiting for

Zachow's Tavern. Photo credit Andrew Sigwell.

the plant to start back up? Zachow's Tavern was just about 100 yards away from the plant, and they sold so much beer that night they needed to send out for more. Many employees drank too much (the majority did not). Management decided at about 7:30 p.m. to not start up the line for the rest of the shift.

This entire incident made management in Janesville and Detroit unhappy. However, my management sources tell me that this episode was not a factor in the decision to move the medium-duty truck to Flint in 2004. (Gambling or drug incidents weren't factors in the move either. Many GM plants had similar issues.) A small number of unidentified employees set off the tear gas. About 2,000 employees had nothing to do with the incident, but hundreds took advantage of the emptying of the plant to drink a lot of beer. Production continued the next day.

Any history of GM and Janesville would be remiss to not include Zachow's Tavern, today the Zoxx 411 Club. This bar (and until 1999 also a restaurant) is located at 411 S. Jackson Street in Janesville, but its location is much better known as "the tavern in the middle of the GM parking lot." The north part of the relatively small tavern was constructed from an old railroad boxcar!

It has a storied history (the name was changed to Zoxx in 2005). GM management in both Janesville and Detroit were never happy with the bar's location less than 100 yards from the plant's front door and surrounded by the plant's parking lots. The problem was that Zachow's was there first. There are varying stories of GM trying to buy the tavern to get rid of it, and rumors of how much was offered. Yet, nearly eleven years after the plant closed, the tavern is still open for business.

Zachow's occupied its present location around 1950. At the time, there were no parking lots, only houses. GM bought all those properties as they needed space for more parking lots. Zachow's was not located there to end up surrounded by parking lots. GM created the situation. They probably figured they'd one day buy Zachow's, but it didn't happen.

Workers had 30-minute lunch breaks, so they needed to get out of the plant and get to Zachow's, pick up their food order, down one or more beers, and get back to their job in a half hour.

Andrew Sigwell, the current owner of Zoxx, is a third-generation proprietor. He told me what it was like when the workers arrived to pick up their food orders. They had about six minutes in the tavern. Sigwell called it "the busiest six minutes in any tavern." There is a photo in this book showing the "scene" during the six minutes. The sandwiches were already prepared, as most of the workers were regulars whose orders could be made ahead. Andrew said that sometimes a GM worker or two would get behind the bar and help open the beers and serve them as fast as they could. All other customers needed to wait for service during the six minutes. The kitchen closed permanently in 1999. Andrew said the lunch hour crowd was not diminished; there just weren't any sandwich sales.

Andrew said he did not know how much money they made during the two daily six-minute sessions. But he did say that overall, they made three times as much ($3,000) on the days the plant was operating. He also said that second shift was busier than first shift. Younger workers with less seniority were on the second shift and not surprisingly ate and drank more. He also said things got busier as the week went on.

I asked Andrew if many GM retirees still came to the tavern to tell stories and relive those days. He said hardly any at all. His customers are now much younger. He doesn't even open most days until 2 p.m. There were other taverns on Jackson Street near the plant where some GM workers would go for food and a beer or two.

Sitting in Zoxx talking with Andrew and getting a feel for the place has led me to think that the bar was more of an image problem for GM than a real problem. People who wanted to drink would figure out a way with or without Zachow's. Food and alcohol were available just another two blocks away, or in their vehicles.

Andrew has also played another key role unrelated to the tavern. He owns some drones and used them and other cameras to record the demolition of the plant. He spent considerable time on it. Several photos in this book come from his willingness to share them with me.

Going back to 2004, the question remains: Did any of the controversies – tear gas, gambling, beer – factor into GM's decision to move the medium truck line from Janesville?

My research, especially talking to two people who were in management in Janesville in the 1990s, provides an entirely different explanation for the medium truck move.

Here are some facts:

• The medium duty truck was profitable for GM and Janesville was the only place they were being assembled.

- GM wanted a whole new model of the medium-duty truck and it would take two years to make the changes to produce the new version.

- GM's choices were to either stop producing a profitable product for at least two years in Janesville, in order to make the necessary changes on the assembly line for the new product, or keep producing the product nonstop in Janesville and remodel another plant to assemble the new version. When we do the math on the net effect of new jobs for SUV production in the 1990s and the loss of 900 jobs when the medium duty truck was moved to Flint, it shows that Janesville had a net increase of 550 jobs (1450 new SUV jobs minus the loss of 900 medium duty truck jobs).

- Making money was more important to GM than the impact of their decision on any one plant. This was a logical but unpleasant decision at the top of GM in Detroit.

- GM leadership, I was told, also was looking to put more workload in the Flint, Michigan plant.

- The influence of Michigan Congressman John Dingell cannot be discounted on this decision to move workload to Michigan. In the late 1990s, Wisconsin had no member of the Wisconsin delegation with the influence of Dingell. He was a Michigan version of Les Aspin. But Les Aspin was gone.

Another controversy during the '90s involved employees calling in sick. UAW members in Janesville refused to volunteer for overtime in vast numbers on October 14, 1996. Management decided there were not enough workers to operate the second shift, and the line was shut down. Folklore and a misstatement by the plant manager two years later passed along the explanation that workers called in sick that night because they wanted to watch the Green Bay Packers game on television. There was no Packers game that night. I have looked at the 1996 Packer schedule. A shutdown related to a Packers game did occur only once, two years later.

The October 1996 issue was that while operating two ten-hour shifts for four days there was a shortage of workers, which was solved by having workers on both shifts volunteer to work two shifts a day—20 hours a day! These were primarily younger workers who saw a chance to make a lot of money (if you don't mind getting almost no sleep). At $28 an hour and time and a half on the second shift they worked, they were making $700 per day. Most of them didn't take the time to go home. They would sleep for three hours or so in one of the cars on the assembly line. Workers on three hours of sleep working around machinery and heavy equipment was clearly an unsafe situation.

The UAW wanted GM to hire more workers and stop this situation. My conversation with management and union members from that time provide a simple explanation. Management realized that more workers were needed, but a new contract was about to be negotiated, and management wanted to have a "give" in negotiations in exchange for something they wanted. But this October 14 shutdown led to GM announcing the next day that 140 to 150 new workers would be hired. This largely ended the bizarre and dangerous situation.

GM needed more capacity than Janesville to meet the SUV demand. I also believe they did not want to rely on just one plant. This gave the UAW International Union too much power by threatening strikes in Janesville. Their answer was to start also building the SUVs in Arlington, Texas, and Silao, Mexico. They began producing SUVs at these sites beginning in 1998. Arlington had space because they were no longer producing the Chevrolet Caprice.

The decade ended with a GM announcement that Janesville would produce the next generation of SUVs. In 2005 they extended this commitment to 2012.

The handling of the loss of the 900 jobs to Flint with the loss of the medium-duty truck in 2004 is worth explaining. Fifty workers transferred to Flint. The other 850 ended up choosing one of the following: retire with their pensions, take a buyout, go into the "jobs bank" where workers received full pay and did many jobs like community service or work in the plant such as painting, or leave and pursue employment somewhere else.

The end of the 1990s saw GM ask the state for a new road that would be a direct route from the new Avalon Road interchange to the GM property. It was about one mile and would have no cross streets, so the purpose was solely for GM traffic. This meant trucks would now not have to travel on any city streets.

Governor Tommy Thompson and local legislators fully supported the new road, which would cost $12 million split between federal, state, and local funds. In fact, the governor came to Janesville to sign the bill authorizing the road into law.

However, once again, GM management behavior spoke volumes. No GM management attended the bill signing although it took place about three blocks from the plant. Local GM management who were working there at the time told me that this nonappearance at the bill signing was a direct order from Detroit.

So again, like GM Detroit's reaction to the taxpayers paying for the interchange in the mid-1980s, GM would not make itself available to the media. They did not want to answer the question about whether this new road would lead to some new signal about GM's future in Janesville.

It should be noted that in 1999 GM had committed to build the new generation of the full-sized SUV through 2005. The new road would be named Reuther Way by the City Council thanks in part to the efforts of City Councilman Tom Brien, who was a UAW worker.

Still, even with GM executives a no-show at the road bill signing, the dawn of the 21st century found the Janesville plant's future looking good, or at least as good as it could look in this volatile, up and down industry. The auto industry is not "recession-proof" like industries that produce essentials of life. People can put off buying a new vehicle for a year or more if they must. Overall, Janesville ended one century and started a new one assured of at least five more years of work. A few years later GM extended their commitment from 2005 to 2012. Job security looked good. SUV sales were skyrocketing. In 2004, GM announced plans to invest $175 million to reboot the Janesville plant for the new truck production.

Those were good times. However, they didn't last. ıl

🔟
Final Curtain: What We Didn't Know Made All the Difference

Past is often prologue. The story of the auto/truck industry has been since 1923 consistently inconsistent. History has told us many times to not take the future for granted because things are going well today.

Welcome to 2005. Big vehicle sales started to slump. GM announced in November 2005 that it intended to close 12 plants and cut 30,000 jobs by 2008. But Janesville had dodged this bullet. We were not on the list. Janesville was producing a product that earned GM $10,000 per vehicle, but someone had to buy the vehicle to make the profit.

Then Janesville entered 2008. Everything that could go wrong did go wrong. Janesville had been told they would be producing the SUVs until at least 2012.

We went from "everything looks good" in the early 2000s to the plant closing in 2008. The suddenness of this change made the closing even more devastating for everyone. Twelve plants closed in 2007—but not Janesville. The shock of the closing on December 23, 2008, was amplified even more because GM had announced in June 2008 that the plant would close by 2010. We did not think that meant before Christmas 2008. The closing of the plant in 2008 was and is the most damaging economic event in the history of Janesville.

The fateful year of 2008 had dawned with deep concern but also long-held hope that somehow Janesville would survive the multiple problems GM and America faced. After all, GM closed 12 plants in 2007, and Janesville was not one of them. The previous sixteen years had shown that America loved the SUVs Janesville's plant made and that they were very profitable for GM. Though we knew fuel efficiency was going to be an ongoing issue, gas prices that go up can come back down. No one expected the plant would close before Christmas.

The history of our plant since it began making Chevrolets in 1923 was filled with bad news, including production slowdown, layoffs, a temporary (14 month) closing during the Great Depression, a three and a half year production stop to make war materials to win World War II, and the loss of some products, then the awarding of new ones. It was understandable to believe we would survive again.

GM's announcement on June 2, 2008, that they intended to close the Janesville plant by 2010 stunned us, but as noted in

Chapter 1, the announcement left open time to do something about it. We thought we had 18 months (at the most) to convince GM to keep the plant open.

As mentioned, in the summer of 2008 Wisconsin Governor Jim Doyle quickly appointed the GM Retention Task Force to put together a financial package to convince GM to stay in Janesville. Governor Doyle, Congressman Ryan, Local 95 President Brad Dutcher, and me, along with other Janesville leaders, were assigned to the task force. The governor asked Brad Dutcher and me to co-chair. At this time in my life I was retired from Blue Cross and serving on the Janesville School Board.

Governor Jim Doyle
Photo credit
Janesville Gazette

Democrats, Republicans, business, and labor united to develop a financial package that would convince GM to stay. We believed our argument was a strong one. To summarize, we emphasized the plant's efficiency, profitability, and good union-management relations. These were significant advantages—in normal times. We didn't realize how abnormal times were, especially for GM.

Without knowledge of GM's impending bankruptcy, we quickly prepared a financial package of over $200 million. It would consist of the following pieces:

- $160 million in tax credits from the state
- $20 million from Rock County
- $15 million from the City of Janesville
- $2 million from the City of Beloit

- $500,000 from the private sector in Janesville (to be used to buy out the tavern in the GM parking lot and replace it with a daycare center for employees' children)
- Unquantified subsidies for GM for health care costs and utility costs

I am sure many reading this in 2019 will compare the $200 million in 2008 with former Governor Walker's potentially $4 billion incentive to attract Foxconn to Wisconsin in 2018. All I can say is that this was a competitive number at the time, and many feel the $4 billion was indefensible from the taxpayers' standpoint.

We met with GM in Detroit and presented our case, but the GM plant in Janesville would be closed on December 23, 2008, with only 10 weeks notice, and just three months after our Detroit meeting.

What we did not know made all the difference. We did not know there was a second meeting in Washington, D.C. the same week as our Detroit meeting which was far more important to GM. In fact, the subject matter of the Washington meeting made our Detroit meeting unlikely to influence GM's plans to close Janesville. The two meetings taking place at nearly the same time is best described as two ships passing in the night.

We were arguing to keep one plant open. But General Motors, the second largest manufacturing company in the United States and maybe the most famous manufacturing company in the world for at least 70 years, was going broke at a lightning-fast pace and possibly facing bankruptcy. Mighty General Motors!

The gathering in Washington involved GM CEO Rick Wagoner meeting with George W. Bush Administration officials to discuss GM's disastrous financial situation. The GM contingent was encouraging the Bush Administration to support a bailout that would cost American taxpayers $25 billion. During 2008, GM was losing billions every *quarter*! GM was publicly traded, so the public knew they were losing money, but Wagoner recognized that projections for future quarters might involve even more billions of dollars. The future of the Janesville plant was the last thing on Wagoner's mind.

This was occurring at the same time as the subprime financial crisis on Wall Street, which would lead to a federal bailout costing more billions of dollars.

It is worth mentioning that in the fall of 2008, the Bush Administration was about to be a lame duck as America would pick a new president in November. President-elect Barack Obama said that America had only one president at a time, so GM continued to pursue bailout help with the outgoing Bush Administration until it left on January 20, 2009.

While many criticized GM for the apparent cold-heartedness of closing the Janesville plant two days before Christmas, we don't know what pressure GM was under from the Bush Administration to show that they were serious about cutting costs. It is worth noting that much of the Janesville SUV production would go to Arlington, Texas. This was a logical place to consolidate SUV production as Arlington was already producing SUVs. It's also true it was the home state of President Bush and where he was retiring when he left office.

Steven Rattner's book *Overhaul* tells the story of General Motors' financial condition in late 2008. Until fall 2008, GM employees and citizens of Janesville knew nothing of this possible, impending bankruptcy that Rattner states GM management fought against well into 2009. Rattner makes clear that GM top management did not want to go through bankruptcy and then be forced to operate a more efficient GM so the taxpayers that saved GM had the chance to get their money back. The Obama Administration ultimately made them do it.

As I noted in Chapter 1, I was at the plant on December 23, 2008, the saddest day in history for Janesville's economy and thousands of workers and their families. But along with sorrow, I felt pride, and I believe others did, too, for the 85 years of assembling millions of vehicles in our city. Many of us likely were pondering a similar question where this sad ending was concerned. Had the management and union in Janesville really had any control of their destiny? A history lesson may prove helpful here.

The relationship between GM management and the UAW since the 1930s is full of contentious fights, strikes, and promises to work together in the future. A century of knowledge about the auto industry tells of constant struggle between management and employees with fights, plant layoffs and shutdowns, strikes, etc.

The negative but often accurate view of management in the early 20th century can be summarized by saying that management believed workers had no rights in "their" company. Union organizers had little respect for management, and management hiring people to literally beat up or even shoot the organizers certainly didn't help.

Both sides had decades of trouble accepting the wisdom of one of Walter Reuther's famous quotes, "Labor and management have a lot more in common than they realize." I earlier described a moment in 1986 when local management and UAW Local 95 in Janesville believed the words of Reuther, and very good things happened for the plant, the employees, and the community.

A list of the most significant factors that impacted the ups and downs of the industry shows that local management and the union had no power to alter or prevent those events from happening. Let me list some of them:

- National recessions: These always hurt the industry because people could go without a new car or truck during a downturn. These led to layoffs at many employers.

- The Great Depression of the 1930s: The Depression deeply hurt the industry, and Janesville saw several shutdowns and layoffs when line speed slowed down to reflect the need to produce fewer vehicles. The longest shutdown lasted over one year between September 1932 and late 1933.

- Adolf Hitler: America had to devote all its efforts to defeat the Nazis and then Japan. The auto industry played a huge role. The plants stopped making vehicles between April 1942 and the end of 1945. They were converted to produce tanks, planes, jeeps, weapons, and ammunition. They were called the "arsenal of democracy." Wages were frozen, but profits for the companies were very substantial. Victory in Europe and Asia during 1945 led to over three decades of great prosperity in America and the auto industry. This did not occur without major fights between the UAW and GM. Workers wanted pay raises to compensate for years of frozen wages during the war while GM made profits.

- Japanese competition comes to America: Their cars were well-built and were more fuel-efficient than the larger GM products. The Japanese automakers also started building plants in America. I should mention that GM management in Detroit took its time responding to the Japanese competition.

- Technology, especially robots: Neither GM nor the UAW could stop progress or change. These changes helped GM be more efficient and profitable but at the cost of jobs.

- Gasoline prices: Spikes in gas prices were always going to hurt less fuel-efficient vehicles like the SUVs assembled in Janesville from 1991 until the plant closed in 2008. GM could have aggressively developed more fuel-efficient, smaller vehicles, but that may not have helped Janesville unless they had assigned the production to Janesville. When gas prices rose in 2006 and 2007 and then reached $4 per gallon in 2008, SUV sales tanked. Neither management nor the UAW had any impact on OPEC.

- GM ties to the Defense Department: GM had significant contracts with the Defense Department, and that gave Les Aspin clout with GM regarding the Janesville plant. He played a key role in getting new products assigned to Janesville in the late 1980s. The UAW played a significant role in his primary victory in his first run for Congress in 1970. They supported him in his re-election efforts and were helpful with other members of Congress in his rise to chairman. But it would be a stretch to say that either the UAW or GM played a decisive role in his rise to chairman. Aspin, however, died in 1995.

Though the historic agreement of 1986 did help with the decision by GM to assign more products to Janesville for a time, the above factors, and those below, ultimately won out. The UAW and local GM management also had no control over GM Detroit and their financial decisions. In *Overhaul,* Steve Rattner minces no words in describing the serious problems at GM's highest level.

Quoting from *Overhaul,* "Everyone involved agreed that a total overhaul [of GM] was necessary [if it was to have a chance to be profitable post-bankruptcy].... The 'viability plan' devised by GM in February 2009 had proven management incapable of dispassionately and analytically creating an achievable business plan.... GM was an antique, closed corporate structure.... The company's problems were, to a considerable degree, of its own making—and fixable."

Harry Wilson was the key person on the Obama Administration team specifically assigned to fix GM. His job was to develop "a sensible plan to end GM's decades-long pattern of careening from crisis to crisis."

Obama's people asked the CFO of GM how much cash the company needed to operate the company day to day. The CFO, Ray Young, told them $11 billion. Wilson thought that was way too high. It turned out the correct answer was $6 billion. The CFO was 4 to 5 billion dollars off! This is not a "down in the weeds" question to the CFO. It was a "30,000-foot" question that the CFO should have automatically had in his head.

Rattner wrote that they found a "decrepit" financial system. For example, a GM advisor told Rattner's team, "No one had a list of all of the GM bank accounts worldwide." Rattner noted GM also had big problems with its accounting operation. In March 2006, GM announced it had to revise its profit figures for the previous six years because of questionable accounting.

GM had eight separate vehicles with 45 models in the U.S.— too many and not enough differentiation in the marketplace. By comparison, Toyota had only two brands. Think of Buick, Oldsmobile, and Pontiac, and try to make clear distinctions as a consumer. Everyone could see and describe the differences between a Chevrolet and a Cadillac.

If you do not read all of *Overhaul,* I urge you to at least read the chapter entitled, "Harry Wilson's War." It should irritate you, and if you were one of the tens of thousands of employees who lost your job, it would likely make you beyond angry.

One can make a strong case that the GM collapse, which played a big part in their need to close the Janesville plant and 27 others, was the result of the leadership's incompetence at the top of GM. They survived that incompetence until strong Japanese competition and rising gas prices showed up.

GM's problems, which Rattner describes in detail, are listed with brevity here:

- GM had too much capacity (plants and floor space), which cost money. It is likely that if Janesville had not been closed in 2008, it would have been closed during the bankruptcy in 2009 with less generous buyouts, etc. than workers received in 2008.

- GM had bad deals with their suppliers, and this wasted money.

- GM had too many dealers when measured by vehicles sold per dealership compared to their competitors, which cost money.

- GM's deal with these dealers cost a lot of money to get out of.

- GM's board would not discuss budget items that had a cost below one billion dollars! Rattner points out this meant that bills (costs) of $600 million, $900 million, never received the board's attention. The bills were just paid, and this situation was known outside of GM.

What could Local 95 or Janesville management have done about any of this? An event such as the closing of the plant in 2008 inevitably prompted people to look for reasons, causes, and scapegoats. This is still a source of discussion 10 years later.

No one in Janesville can be blamed for this situation. Detroit GM gave Janesville profitable but not fuel-efficient vehicles, and the good times rolled from the early 1990s to almost 2006. We sought the products GM had available for assignment to a new plant. If GM had fuel-efficient vehicles to assign Janesville in 1987 and 1989, then we would have been assembling them in 2008. But they didn't, and we were always ecstatic to get the products we won.

Many still wonder why they left. Could it have been saved? Could they have been persuaded to stay? Who might have persuaded them to stay? Who could have bullied them or had the clout to muscle them into staying? Did anyone not try hard enough? Most of these questions have answers.

I am writing this part of the book in fall 2018. The North American Free Trade Agreement (NAFTA) is in the news as President Trump has made our trade agreements with countries all over the world a big issue. Many Americans are unhappy and even disgusted with NAFTA and our trade policies that have played a role in American jobs moving to other countries. This book is not about broad conclusions concerning this issue.

Look at where the lost jobs from Janesville went. Most of them went to Fort Wayne, Indiana, in 1986; Flint, Michigan, in 2004; and Arlington, Texas, in 2008. A small percentage of SUV production went to Mexico in 2008. Our job losses were almost all to another location in the United States. The closing of the Janesville plant had nothing to do with NAFTA or American trade policy over the last 30 years.

Why did they leave? The known facts from GM are pretty clear. Many factors played a role:

• Like all companies, sales and profits matter. Profits at the Janesville plant were very, very good. A $10,000 profit was made on each SUV. They produced one per minute totaling $600,000 per hour, and with two 10-hour shifts, the profit was $12 million per day. But if gas prices go up and people stop buying SUVs, everything changes. GM was also assembling these vehicles in Arlington, Texas, and Silao, Mexico. Gas prices went up to over $4 per gallon in 2008. Sales slumped badly and GM had a big problem—overcapacity. SUVs had stopped selling, and they didn't need two plants producing them. GM had let the overcapacity problem get out of hand. They had closed 12 plants in 2007 and three more in 2008 in addition to Janesville. Then they closed 12 more plants during the 2009 bankruptcy. GM may have been able to ride out this slump if they were not going broke.

- We now see that GM believed they needed to close a plant producing SUVs. Would it be Arlington or Janesville? I could find no one who believed closing the Mexico plant was ever considered. The plant in Mexico largely produced vehicles to be sold in other countries, not the U.S.

Janesville vs. Arlington for SUVs:

Janesville had good quality and profit per vehicle. Janesville was more pro-union than Arlington, and it was an older plant, built in 1919 for Sampson Tractor and then switched to GM car production in 1923.

GM concluded that a modern paint shop was better. A paint shop is a bigger deal than any outsider would likely think. It is one of the four main assembly areas (body shop, paint shop, trim shop, and chassis). Arlington's paint shop was more modern than Janesville's. It could apply three different colors on a vehicle, and Janesville could only do two. A new paint shop for Janesville (which was deemed essential by GM if they were to stay in Janesville) would cost an estimated $800 million. They already had the one they needed in Arlington.

Texas had a larger and more powerful congressional delegation than Wisconsin, and it was the home of the president of the United States whom they had begun negotiating with for the federal bailout.

Texas was also a much larger market for the SUV than Wisconsin. They called them "Texas Cadillacs!" This reduced shipping costs.

- "What GM giveth, GM can taketh away." They had taken the medium-duty truck from Michigan to Janesville in 1987. In the early 2000s they gave it back to the Flint, Michigan, plant. Michigan, the home of GM, UAW, and with a strong congressional delegation, had cards that Janesville could not match. With GM going broke, they were already thinking "federal bailout." The human element can't be ignored. GM and UAW leadership were living in a state with several closed plants and thousands of laid-off workers. They saw the closed plants, and they heard from the workers.

Could GM have been persuaded to stay? The battle to save the plant in Janesville, against the background of GM's impending bankruptcy, was fought with merits and what political clout we had to force GM to conclude that they should stay in Janesville with some product.

First, the merits (there is always a chance they will matter). GM acknowledged that Janesville was efficient, largely due to the 1986 contract changes, and the plant produced SUVs at a per vehicle cost lower than Arlington. These merits were obviously not enough.

So, who had political clout?

- Governor Jim Doyle did his best, but GM cared more about politicians in Washington. They had defense contracts to protect, and they needed $25 billion. Governors do not control defense contracts and do not have $25 billion. Also, if GM left Wisconsin, they would have no factories in the state, so they had no fear (or need) of Wisconsin leaders going forward.

- Congressman Paul Ryan was, in 2008, a backbencher in the minority party and would not be the speaker for seven more years.

- There was no one in the Wisconsin congressional delegation in key leadership positions that mattered to GM.

- The UAW International Union had no one at or near the top with close ties to Janesville. Dennis Williams came out of our region and eventually reached the presidency of the UAW, but that occurred after the plant had been closed.

- President Barack Obama was still president-elect when the plant closed. I devote a whole chapter on his role in this, particularly the decisions he made when he was bailing out GM with over $50 billion of tax money and taking them through bankruptcy.

- I cannot prove the role of lame-duck President George W. Bush. The SUVs went to his home state of Texas. But that was the only other plant in the country that was producing SUVs, so he hardly could have been muscling GM to send the SUVs there, although he might have wanted it done while he was still president. This could explain the sudden closing of the plant with just 10 weeks notice on December 23, just before his presidency came to an end.

- The other obvious player was GM Detroit. It seems to me the conclusion is that they had far bigger problems than the future of one plant, and moving most of the workload to Arlington is what they wanted and what President Bush would have liked. Our clout was not enough.

Those of us working to convince GM to keep the Janesville plant open knew there was a good chance that GM would not leave the SUV production in Janesville. We were fighting to keep the plant open and be awarded the assembly of the Chevy Spark. The Spark was a small, fuel-efficient vehicle. Our major competition was Michigan and South Korea. The effort continued into 2009. Michigan, of course, won. Why?

- No congressional leaders from Wisconsin had a position of power that GM cared about. We no longer had a Les Aspin in Washington.

- Michigan, on the other hand, had a larger and more influential congressional delegation. Their most powerful member was Congressman John Dingell. He served from 1955 through 2014—longer than any Congressman in the nation's history. He died in February 2019 at age 92 while I was finishing this book. His importance to GM can hardly be overstated. He was the longtime chairman of the House Energy and Commerce Committee. This committee had jurisdiction over a huge range of issues including issues vitally important to the auto industry such as clean air legislation, auto emission regulation, and miles per gallon requirements. He was once asked the extent of his committee's jurisdiction over issues, and he said, "If it moves, it's energy, and if it doesn't move, it's commerce." Wisconsin's entire congressional delegation in 2008 and 2009 likely did not have as much clout with the auto industry as Energy and Commerce Chairman John Dingell. It is no surprise that we did not get the replacement Chevy Spark. It went to Michigan.

- Michigan had better connections at the leadership level of the UAW International Union than Janesville did. Until 1987, we had the late Ray Majerus, secretary-treasurer of the UAW International Union (the number two position), a great leader at the UAW. He was close to Local 95. I knew him as a state senator in the late 1970s and 1980s when he was leader of Region 10 of the UAW, which included Wisconsin. He died too young, at 63, in 1987.

When considering all the above points (and with the benefit of hindsight), the overwhelming conclusion is that we were not going to win. Now that GM is gone for good from Janesville, I have looked back over the 85 years (1923–2008) that GM was in Janesville and see the warning signs.

For at least the last 40 years in Janesville GM "rented" our city. They showed on multiple occasions that they could be persuaded to stay or muscled into staying when we had the late Congressman Les Aspin on our side. But no long-term security was ever really given by GM. This was also true for many other plants in the auto industry.

GM executives at the plant never played consistent roles in the Janesville community. None ever served on the school board or city council like leaders of many other businesses. Put another way, GM dated Janesville for a long time but never married. Janesville was finally left standing alone at the altar in 2008.

GM played Janesville. We were never going to win. We fought the fight we had to fight. Between GM and its supplier plants in Janesville, 4,500 jobs (4,500 families) were at stake. This was real. Only afterward was it clear that we were fighting with one hand tied behind our back.

GM overcapacity eventually led to the closing of 28 plants. We were one of them. **ıl**

The end. The iconic 100-year-old smokestack comes down to join the rubble that is left of the plant. Photo credit Janesville Gazette.

11

Obama and Janesville

Former President Barack Obama played a part in the Janesville-GM story. He did so as a candidate for president during the Wisconsin Democratic primary in early 2008 and then again as the president who decided to use the power of the government to save GM and use billions of dollars of taxpayer money to make that happen. There was hope he would also save the Janesville plant.

In the opening chapter I referenced February 13, 2008, when Senator Obama was running against Hillary Clinton in the Wisconsin Democratic primary. He gave a speech on the economy at the Janesville GM plant. It was near the time GM would announce their intention to

President Barack Obama
Photo credit
Janesville Gazette

close the plant by 2010. Gas prices were on their way to $4 per gallon, sales of the large SUVs made in Janesville had shrunk, and GM had closed 12 other plants in 2007.

Obama spoke to a large audience of hundreds of UAW workers and GM management and people from the community, including me. The workers were scared to death over the impending loss of their jobs. I have included a transcript of Obama's entire speech in the appendix.

His speech lifted the spirits of the crowd. He said that the economy he wanted to help build in America would mean the Janesville plant "will be here" for another 100 years. The crowd cheered! However, I would encourage you to read the entire speech. My view is he did not express the kind of commitment to Janesville if he was elected president that I and many others had hoped to hear. He did not say something like the following: "If I am elected, I will not let GM close this plant." There was no firm pledge to keep it open. Should a presidential hopeful say that? In the big picture, I do not think so. But as a guy from Janesville with so many friends and their families relying on that plant for a job, I sure wish he would have.

President Obama decided to use over $50 billion of taxpayer money to save both Chrysler and GM. Could he have sent a message to GM to reopen Janesville? Sure, but he didn't. However, Rattner's book makes it clear that the president was firm in his demand that they had two goals: to save GM and to do it in a way that the new GM would be profitable, assuring that everything is done to retrieve the taxpayer money. So the new GM was created with fewer than half of all GM properties. One hundred twenty-one properties were put in new GM and 127 properties put in old GM, which was named Motors Liquidation Company (MLC). The word *liquidation* made clear the purpose of old GM.

The goal was to get rid of everything in MLC: 127 properties, 48 million square feet of buildings, and billions of dollars of debt. This was done to give the new GM the chance to succeed. New GM had 200,000 workers. If a person or company stops paying their bills, it sure is easier to get into a much better financial position. That is what new GM did.

One might have expected that the closed Janesville plant would be in old GM's MLC so it could be discarded. It wasn't, however, because of its standby status, along with Spring Hill, Tennessee, and Orion Township, Michigan. Maybe this was the bone Obama threw to Janesville. I haven't had the chance to talk to him. Janesville was assigned standby status in May 2009, which was right in the middle of the bankruptcy process.

This discussion of President Obama's role in the Janesville GM plant saga has made me realize that Senator Hillary Clinton played no role at all. During that primary, in February 2008, Senator Clinton never campaigned in Janesville, nor did she campaign in Wisconsin during the general election in 2016. She was the first Democratic candidate for president to lose Wisconsin since 1984.

Was her decision to not come to Janesville in the 2008 primary against Obama a precursor to her campaign decision to decide not to come to Wisconsin (let alone Janesville) in the 2016 general election? It's certainly worth considering.

Why didn't she come to Janesville in the 2008 primary? Janesville is a city of 60,000 that is also 60 percent Democratic and full of Democrats of both genders who supported her husband. Many Democrats would have loved to come out to see and meet Hillary Clinton, former U.S. senator and first lady, and the most serious woman candidate for president in the history of the country. She had support in Janesville in the presidential primary.

I think Senator Obama's Janesville speech in the appendix was brilliant. It was a call to action for the federal government to insert itself into the American economy on behalf of the average American, which he described in understandable terms. He contrasted this by mentioning the many ways the federal government had protected and aided already well-off Americans.

Senator Obama's speech included a broad list of actions he would take as president. His specific references to the situation in the Janesville plant were made after he laid out his economic agenda for a nation facing the housing crisis, the financial institutions crisis, national recession, job losses to overseas countries, the need for minimum wage increases, protections for people gouged on their loans, the need for a clean energy economy, and other issues he would address as president. Then he said the following about the Janesville plant:

> I know that General Motors received some bad news yesterday, and I know how hard your governor has fought to keep jobs in this plant. But I also know how much progress you've made—how many hybrids and fuel-efficient vehicles you're churning out. And I believe that if our government is there to support you and give you the assistance you need to retool and make this transition, that this plant will be here for another hundred years.

The words in the above quote that lifted the spirits of those of us who heard it were, "And I believe that if our government is there to support you and give you the assistance you need to retool and make this transition [to a clean, renewable energy future], that this plant will be here for another hundred years."

His key words were "100 years." Those words inspired the workers. I was there. They inspired me! But those words were not the definitive commitment to keep the plant open that we wanted to hear. People can question whether a candidate's words are appropriate or even believable. President Obama is the only major figure that played a role in the GM-Janesville plant both before and after the plant closed.

When I began to write about the role the former president played and could have played regarding the future of the plant, I thought I would end up writing about great disappointment in him. I began with a simple opinion. It went like this: Senator Obama came to Janesville to get our votes in the 2008 Democratic presidential primary. He gave us what sounded like a commitment to the Janesville plant. He then became president and approved $60 billion of taxpayer money to save GM. Those of us in Janesville believed when he did that in 2009, he could have mentioned to GM leaders, "Just one little thing... reopen that Janesville plant."

As I learned more about the big picture, however, I have concluded it would have been completely contrary to the situation the president faced. He had an obligation to force GM to become efficient so that there was a more likely chance that the taxpayer billions would be paid back by GM.

This GM efficiency included the need to reduce their excessive overcapacity of plant space. Twelve plants were closed in 2007. Janesville and three other plants were closed in 2008, and then 12 more plants were closed during the bankruptcy process in 2009. The president had supporters and friends at all 28 plants. He was asking GM to reduce capacity. How would he ever explain to workers affected by those other 27 closings, "Sorry about the tens of thousands of you. I will do nothing for you, but I will save this one closed plant in Janesville." He could not do that. Those others were his friends and supporters, too.

I'm a Janesville guy. I know so many families directly affected by the closing and many others hurt by the impact the closing had on the rest of the Janesville economy. I end up, however, not being able to criticize the president. I am startled by GM's top leadership over several decades. Their fundamental belief seemed to be that, "we are General Motors, and therefore we can never fail," regardless of their unwillingness to make any tough decisions while they lost huge market share in America, had too many dealers, too many plants, too much in legacy costs compared to their new competition, poor deals with their suppliers, etc. I do not believe they would be as well off today if the Obama administration had not forced them to get their house in order to get their bailout.

Think about it. The government forcing the private sector to be efficient! I'm sure at least 90 percent of Americans would assume the private sector is the efficient one.

I wish President Obama had forced GM to reopen the Janesville plant. He could have, but he didn't. I understand why he didn't, and I do not blame him.

I noticed, however, that the president may have a small level of guilt over not reopening the Janesville plant. Why do I say this? Because in eight years as president he never appeared in Janesville or Rock County despite coming to Wisconsin on at least eight occasions. He came to Madison. Janesville is only 50 minutes away by car. He never came.

Still, reflecting on Barack Obama's election as the first African American president makes this an excellent time to introduce John Scott, Jr., the third African American employee at GM in Janesville, who stands tall as one of the heroes in this narrative. ▎▍

⑫
Race

John Scott, Jr. was born in Indiana in 1911 and died in Janesville in 1993. His wife, Mildred, died in 2006. The story of Scott, the third black person hired by GM in Janesville, particularly after he and his family moved to Janesville in 1948, is a story of racism in Janesville and at General Motors during the 1940s and 1950s, and the beginning of progress in the 1960s.

It is also the story of John's incredible ability to keep his eye on the ball despite all the unpleasant situations he faced. His goal was to have his family live peacefully in Janesville, get work to support them, and

John Scott, Jr. and Mildred Scott

make friends. It is also the story of several kind, open-minded people who treated the Scotts with decency, gave help when they needed it, and supported them when others wouldn't.

John gave an amazing interview in 1976. There are several relevant parts of that interview in the appendix. The Wisconsin State Historical Society conducted the interview as part of a bicentennial project honoring the 200 years since the signing of the Declaration of Independence.

John wanted to buy a home in Janesville in 1948. The unwritten rules were that black people could not rent a place in Janesville. They could only buy a home. So John found a home he wanted to buy on West Eastern (what a name!) Avenue. It is now named Delavan Drive. The realtor, who John liked, said that before he could buy the home, he needed to visit with a few people (all white) who lived close to that house to see if they would approve of the Scott family living there. Did John erupt with anger about this "requirement?" No, he proceeded to visit with these folks he hoped would be his future neighbors. He said the following in his 1976 interview:

> So, anyway, I went to three or four houses and knocked on the door and come to find out that they were railroad men, too [Scott worked for the railroad at this time]... And we sat there... they didn't look at my color, and we had... I had coffee and donuts. And we just set there and talked as if we had known each other all our lives. They said, "Well, what's the difference if you are colored, or if you are a negro. You're a human just like we... just like we are."

One of the neighbors, a woman, said, "If you feel like you ought to live in Janesville, you have as much right to live here in Janesville as anyone else."

John then experienced some additional Janesville kindness. The owners of the home wanted to sell it for $3,500. John told them he only had $1,500, so the owners accepted $1,500 as a down payment.

John then did not have the money to move his belongings from Chicago to his new home. John stopped at J & W Transfer and Storage, a moving company that still operates in Janesville, and as he said, "I just gave them my story. I said I would pay them when I get the money, so they told me not to worry about a thing. They said, 'We'll have our trucks down the second day of January, so you just have everything ready, and you worry about the money later on.' So that's how we got to Janesville."

Scott said, "There was a coal yard, and the fellow that owned that was named William Hill. He came over the next morning after we came here... we had just about a bushel of briquette, and down in the house we had an old coal furnace... we didn't have much fuel. So (Mr. Hill) came over and asked, 'Need anything?'

I said, 'We need so much, but we don't have any money.'

Mr. Hill said, 'Well, don't worry about the money, I'll fill your coal bin up.' I don't know how many tons he put in there, but he just filled it up. He never said anything about the money. So I got a job at the Janesville Country Club."

How Did the Scotts get to Janesville? They were crammed into a one-room apartment in Chicago, and John was working in the dining car on the Chicago and Northwestern Railroad (C & NW) that ran between Chicago and Janesville and onto Minneapolis.

While working, Scott met a couple from Janesville who often took the train to Chicago to bet on horses at the racetrack. One time the man asked John how many children he had. John told him three. The man said, "We had pretty good luck at the racetrack today. Here's some money for the children." John said it was a nice gift. He started talking to them, and they said, "Why not try moving to Janesville?" It was that conversation that brought the Scott family to the city.

John was asked if he recollected any discrimination connected with his work with the C & NW. John said, "No, I did not run into any discrimination." John said in 1976, "We are very happy. I'm not sorry today that I ever came to Janesville."

It took 13 years, until 1961, to finally get hired at GM. During that time, he was always employed, usually on the C & NW train line but also at the Janesville Country Club, Beloit Iron Works, and at Hunter's Motors.

John said he did not experience any discrimination while working for C & NW, but he was also asked, "What about living in Janesville? Did life in Janesville live up to your expectations?" John replied, "Yes, yes, it lived up to it. We took part in everything. What helped an awful lot here were church people." The family belonged to the First Baptist Church. He said they were fully accepted in a predominantly white church. John became the usher captain, and his wife sang in the choir.

John offered some advice to other people of color moving to predominantly white cities. "If you expect to become part of their community, you're going to have to join their organizations, join their churches, get acquainted with school faculty. There is your start right there."

John did say that he experienced discrimination at a tavern where he went with some white coworkers. The bartender did not want to serve John. The fellow with John said to the bartender (who was also the owner), "If Scotty isn't good enough to drink in here, then we are not good enough to drink in here either." Then they left.

John also joined the Masonic Lodge in Beloit in the late 1950s, and that would later play a part in his getting hired at General Motors.

John said the first black hired at GM was Al Beck, who was hired a few years before John. Al was let go just a few weeks before he had served his six-month probation period. John said that Al told him he "got let out of there because of his race."

Al's son Eric told me that his father's hair was not curly like most black people and that his skin was lighter. It appears that GM did not know they were hiring a black man. This is the best-known explanation of how he got hired and then why he was fired. There is no known record stating that Al was given any other reasonable explanation.

Al told John he met his former foreman on the street, and the foreman told Al, "I'm sorry to see you go. You were a good worker. But you know, I'm just a foreman there." Al told John he had no hard feelings against the foreman. This all tells me that the strong views of Walter Reuther had not penetrated the UAW in Janesville in the 1950s. That would soon change dramatically.

I should mention that I am a longtime friend of Al's son, Eric, who is a successful insurance agent in Janesville. He confirmed to me the above descriptions of how his dad was fired. Eric Beck graduated from Janesville High School and still lives there. He is a popular man in town with many friends, and most of them are white. There is no question that Janesville accepts and likes Eric, which is a welcome change from the way his father was treated in the 1950s at GM.

Eric said that his dad moved on with his life after he was fired from GM. He had a horse farm and worked at the Chrysler plant about 40 miles south of Janesville. Al died in 1987 of congenital heart failure at age 57. Al didn't discuss his feelings about his firing with young Eric except to say, "Well, if I can't make it here, I'll make it someplace else." Are you as impressed as I am with his determination to move on, to be bigger than the people who were cruelly unfair to him?

John Scott believed that there was an unwritten local agreement between management and the union not to hire blacks at the GM plant. But he applied for the job at GM anyway. John said about applying, "Everybody there in the office treated me nice. But I knew the score." When asked what he meant by "the score," he said, "I knew they had a discrimination contract there. It was local and not national [there was no way Walter Reuther would have allowed that in a national or local agreement. It had to be unwritten]. And that is why I was not hired [he said he had applied several times in the 1950s and was never hired]."

John tried to get a copy of the local agreement but was never given one. This was before the two unions merged in 1969. John tried to get the contract from both Local 95 and Local 121. He decided to approach Elmer Yenney, the Local 121 president. John said about talking with Yenney, "He got a little bit nasty. This was the one and only time that I really have been insulted here in Janesville. He said to me, 'As long as I am president of Local 121, there will be none of your kind here. To me you are just another Paul Robeson.'"

Who was Paul Robeson? He was a multi-talented black man who went to school at Rutgers and Columbia. He won fifteen letters at Rutgers in four sports and was a two-time football All-American. He then went on to huge success as a singer and actor in plays and movies. He was active in the civil rights movement and was sympathetic toward the Soviet Union. During the Joe McCarthy era in the 1950s he was accused of being a communist and blacklisted. He had his passport taken away for eight years in the 1950s. To be called a Paul Robeson in that era was equated with being a communist, or at least a communist sympathizer, and a troublemaker.

John renewed his application after being encouraged to by two people he knew in GM management. An application would stay on file six months, and then if the applicant was not hired, it would be discarded, and a person would need to fill out a new one to be considered again.

John was finally hired at GM on October 6, 1961. He was the third black person hired at GM. This was a plant with thousands of workers. I was unable to determine who the second black man was. John never mentions him and, since it happened in the 1950s, I could not identify anyone in 2019 who could tell me.

John was asked if he was hired at GM because of a Masonic connection. John said two Masons. When asked if he could be more specific, John just said no. He was upholding a code of secrecy among Masons. So John, a black man, was hired because two white fellow Masons in management helped make it happen.

It is worth noting that Scott was hired on the Fisher Body side of the plant, which meant he worked on the Local 95 side. Elmer Yenney's contemptible pledge survived at Local 121 under his watch.

John Scott did not talk about, nor was he asked about an experience he endured at his barber shop in Janesville. The barber, Phil Parish, was happy to cut John's hair. But he received flak from some white customers about him having a black customer. They said they would find another barber if Parish kept cutting John's hair.

A few words about Phil Parish. He was one of the "Janesville 99," a National Guard unit from Janesville that was called up at the beginning of World War II. They were captured when the Philippines fell to the Japanese in 1942. He survived the infamous Bataan Death March when many captured Americans died. He and the other survivors were shipped to Japan where he was a POW until the war ended in 1945. Phil Parish survived the abuse and poor treatment and came back to Janesville, became a barber, but never forgot what he fought for. He fought for an America that was fair to everyone regardless of the color of their skin plus other values he held dear.

Phil kept cutting John Scott's hair. One day a rock was thrown through the window of his barber shop. His barbershop was at the east end of the Creston Park shopping center. John heard about what happened, so he went to Phil and told him that he did not want to hurt Phil's business and it would be fine if Phil came to John's house and cut his hair there. Phil said insistently, "No way. You keep coming to my shop, and I will cut your hair there. I did not fight in World War II to let America become this kind of place."

John kept getting his hair cut by Phil, and there were no more known incidents. Janesville has changed for the better since that incident. I do not believe this would happen in the Janesville of today. Phil Parish's son Curt told me of his memories of this, although it was the early 1960s and he was a young boy at the time. Curt is a successful businessman in Janesville today.

This example shows a consistent reaction to the insults John faced. He wanted a good job to support his family, and he was willing to turn the other cheek more often than many others of any color would have. He clearly liked people and wanted them to like him. The problem was that the racist people got the attention and unfortunately hurt Janesville's image as a place open to diversity. My research shows that Janesville had lots of Phil Parishes and people like John Scott's new neighbors in 1948, the people at J & W Transfer, John's fellow members of the First Baptist Church, and on and on. But they were not the city leaders. They were not the management and union at the GM plant, nor were they the realtors or the bankers. Hence, the image and reality of our past require current citizens to continue our efforts to show and prove that that was the Janesville of the past, and it is not the Janesville of 2019. I know people and groups of people, churchgoers and people who do not go to church who are all accepting of people regardless of their skin color. It is truly a new Janesville—much better but not yet perfect.

I met with John's son, John Scott III, for an interview on October 25, 2018. He has lived in Janesville since he was a young boy. He is a 1964 graduate of Janesville High School and worked briefly at GM. It took his father 13 years and then the secret help of two fellow Masons in management at GM to get hired. Just three years later, GM wanted his son after he graduated from high school! GM and the union wanted him to work there. It is an interesting coincidence that that was the same year the Civil Rights Act was passed. John Jr. started working, but as he told them, he had committed to serve in the U.S. Navy for four years. He worked the last 23 years of his career as a deputy with the Rock County Sheriff's Department. During the last 19 years there he worked with social workers intervening in child and domestic abuse issues "keeping people out of crisis," as he put it.

I asked John III what he remembered about the haircut incident. He said that in general, his dad "didn't bring the problems he faced into [our] home and have them affect his kids." But he did remember his dad coming home and saying something like, "Phil is having some trouble, and we may need to go back to Beloit to get our haircuts." Beloit, a city just 12 miles south of Janesville, had and has a large black population and barbershops that would welcome them.

John III said his dad worked at GM from about 1962 until around 1968 when he suffered two heart attacks. After his retirement his dad joined the NAACP and became the president of the Janesville chapter. John Jr. lived a long life after he retired from GM. He would speak out on issues while he was president of the NAACP.

John Jr. was living at Riverview Heights when he died in 1993 at age 82. Fred Holt, a former Janesville schools superintendent, started a minority scholarship which was later named after John Scott. It is still going today.

Though it was not his responsibility to do so, I do not doubt that John Scott, Jr.'s personality and demeanor helped change the views of many of the people he met, who in many cases were meeting and getting to know the first black person in their lives.

You have read stories of outright and blatant racism at the GM plant that both management and the UAW were complicit in. Only three black employees were hired between 1923 and 1961! Now it should be acknowledged that during that time Janesville was a nearly all-white community. That was not an accident. However, just 12 miles south of Janesville was the city of Beloit which by the 1930s and even more so the 1940s had a large black population, and Beloit factories were hiring them. But none of them could get hired at GM.

By about 1970, however, the situation had changed. There were still workers with racist views and inappropriate language, but the official attitude of GM management and Local 95 had changed. They started hiring black Americans.

How did this finally happen? Others may have their own explanations, but I believe there were two big reasons: the civil rights movement and the federal legislation that passed in reaction to that movement, and Walter Reuther. The Reuther chapter tells of his public efforts to support the civil rights movement and Dr. Martin Luther King, Jr. But he did something else to change opinions within the union. He had the UAW purchase an education center at Black Lake in northern Michigan in 1967. Since the late 1960s, thousands of UAW members (and their families) have attended classes and seminars on topics including the reason for unions and explanations on what the UAW was doing and why they were doing it, and there was significant attention given to civil rights and racial justice. Reuther died shortly after Black Lake opened, but his strong views on this issue were carried on by successor after successor. It was then the job of attendees to return to their Locals and share what they had learned. Local union presidents were always invited to Black Lake. A person's feelings, emotions, and prejudices seldom change overnight, but they can change over time.

There is a question on my mind and maybe yours, too. How was it that Reuther was a chairperson of the civil rights movement in America as a close ally of Dr. Martin Luther King, Jr., yet he presided over a union that in Janesville for sure and perhaps in other auto plants across America was compliant with management in opposing, delaying, and stopping the hiring of black workers and paying women at GM in Janesville less pay than men until the late 1960s? Reuther had been president of the union since 1946. Did he not know about the unwritten behavior of some of his local union presidents? Did he not want to know? I can't find the answers to these questions. I also do not doubt Reuther's commitment to equality in America and civil rights for all and specifically in the 1960s.

My guess is that he saw the need to bring equality to all Americans, not just within his union. This nationwide approach to a problem by Reuther would have been consistent with his nation and worldwide approach to raising the retirement income of all Americans through his efforts to get Social Security increases and through his involvement in the issue of protecting and saving our environment.

I believe his approach was not to charge into a town like Janesville and start preaching and trying to impose his views on equal rights for all Americans, but rather to teach it at Black Lake and to change the laws of this nation.

Racism in Janesville is still a difficult topic to discuss in 2019 just as it always has been since the beginning of our nation, and white people are the least likely to want to discuss it.

The story of white racism in Janesville is not pretty and has a long history. It is also important to mention that although this book focuses on the racism toward African Americans specifically at the Janesville GM plant, Janesville also has large Hispanic and Laotian populations who have experienced racism from white Janesville citizens over the years. The good news is that Janesville has made significant progress. We have come a long way, but we (white people in Janesville) must admit we had a long way to come, still have a ways to go, and must keep working toward ending racism in our community.

The racism in the GM plant reflected the racism in the city. The gender bias and male power structure in the plant, management, and union reflected the city's white male power structure.

I am aware that writing about all of this will likely pick a scab, and that some people in Janesville will say racism is over. But I believe a wound must be cleaned to have it heal. Racism in America is as old as when the Europeans first arrived to take the land away from the Native Americans. Then most black people arrived on slave ships. Racism among white people in Janesville and across America is hundreds of years old. America has only addressed it since the 1960s. We have tried to fix in 60 years what was ingrained for hundreds of years. We can't just move beyond it. We must work our way through it. Janesville is getting there.

The Janesville I grew up in and lived in all my life used the N-word commonly. In this almost entirely white city, it could be used openly because people could be almost certain that a black person would not overhear it used because there were no black people to hear it!

Today I still hear stories of people using it in smaller groups and mostly groups of older people. The good news today is that I hear from people that someone in the group is likely to speak up against the language. That is real progress. Even those offended were not likely to say anything 20 or more years ago.

Janesville and its power centers, including GM, spent enormous energy and used their power to keep people of color out of Janesville starting in the 1920s and continuing until at least the 1970s. They succeeded, but at an enormous price. They thought they could keep Janesville 99 percent white forever (or at least for their lifetime).

This is the price Janesville paid. Rather than welcoming black people to Janesville in those decades so we could have, several generations later, a large black middle class, we did not welcome them and now have a huge percentage of people of color who moved here after the 1970s living on low incomes. There is no sizable middle class of people of color in Janesville, but this is changing. Those racists of the past went to their graves with the white Janesville they wanted. But they left a Janesville with poverty that could have been avoided.

The new Janesville city manager in 1976 was a wonderful man named Phil Deaton. He is now retired and living in Wisconsin. I was a state senator then, and he told of the following discussion that took place in his office.

One of the prominent "city fathers" came to see Phil on his first day as the city manager. He was one of those prominent citizens who have a story about them on the front page of the local newspaper when they die. The article would be full of praise for their contributions to Janesville.

This man said to Deaton, "Have you had a chance to drive around Janesville?"

Deaton said, "Yes, just yesterday my wife and I drove around the city looking for a place to live."

This man then asked him, "Did you see any black people?"

Deaton said, "Well, now that you ask, no I didn't."

Then this man delivered his punchline, "We like it that way!"

Deaton also shared a telling story that occurred when he was singing in the choir at his church. There was one black man in the congregation, and he was listening to the choir along with the rest of the congregation.

While the choir was between songs, a man standing next to Deaton said about the black man, "Look at that. That is going to be trouble!" This from a person who sings in a church choir on Sunday morning. This is another discouraging example of the Janesville of some 35 years ago.

Deaton had worked in Ayden, North Carolina, prior to coming to Janesville. He told me the racial makeup of Ayden was about 50-50 black and white. He said nearly half of the white citizens belonged to the KKK. This was clear because they wore a KKK pin on their shirt or coat. So when he came to Janesville, he was experienced on racial feelings. He did not expect to find such racism in a northern city.

Phil Deaton is one of the finest public servants I have ever known. He is dedicated to his job, exhibits the highest ethical standards, and is a model for everyone in public office.

Following is one of Dr. Martin Luther King, Jr.'s most famous quotes. It is from his August 1963 "I Have a Dream" speech at the Lincoln Memorial: "I have a dream that my four little children will one day live in a nation where they will not be judged by the color of their skin, but by the content of their character." With each succeeding generation, Janesville is pursuing Dr. King's dream. One of Dr. King's other quotes was, "The moral arc of the universe is long, but it bends toward justice." So does the moral arc of Janesville. The city is becoming more integrated.

Today about 27 percent of Janesville's school population are students of color. My class of 1962 had two students of color out of 430. I first encountered people of color when I was 15 and met Tim and Loretta Davis in tenth grade. Today it is highly likely that in Janesville a white kid and a student of color will meet by pre-kindergarten. Our teaching staff is gradually becoming racially diverse. I started a foundation in 2008 to speed this up. I am also convinced that the millennial generation is the most tolerant in American history.

Now let me offer a few words about the Civil Rights Act of 1964 and its impact. At that time, most Americans in the North (including this 20-year-old college kid) thought the purpose of the 1964 Civil Rights Act was to correct injustices in the South and injustices to black Americans.

Most northerners believed the South still had a lot to change 99 years after the end of the Civil War. That was true. But the often-unspoken truth was that the North had to change, too. Specific to this story, Janesville and the GM plant needed to change.

The Civil Rights Act prohibited discrimination in a broad array of private conduct. Title VII of the Act "prohibited employment discrimination based on race, sex, color, religion, and national origin." In other words, this law made illegal the very actions that GM in Janesville took against black citizens like John Scott and women like Doris Thom.

I view the Act as an attempt to make white Americans better human beings. This Act intended to make true those famous words from the preamble to the Declaration of Independence. "All men (and women) are created equal," in the South and across all of America.

Things began to change at the GM plant after the Civil Rights Act. Women were able to work assembly line jobs, and their wages were made equal to men's. Also, the plant started hiring black employees. I could not find specific numbers, but one of my biggest helpers in researching this book, Bruce Penny, told me that when he was hired at GM in December 1970, he was in a new group of 18, and he was the only white person. The other 17 were black. Laws do not change attitudes overnight, but they do change actions, and they did change Janesville and GM over time.

The story of Lonnie Brigham, Jr. is worth telling because it involves racism in Janesville in the not too distant past, and how Lonnie fought through to a better Janesville, a better police department, and to a prominent position for Lonnie at the Boys and Girls Club and his service on several advisory committees for the police department and others citywide.

Fifty-four-year-old Lonnie Brigham, Jr. was born and raised in Chicago and moved with his family to Janesville in 2000. He worked as a paralegal in a large Chicago law firm and commuted until 2008, driving to Harvard, Illinois, and

Lonnie grew up in Chicago in a low income neighborhood. He moved to Janesville in 2000 and has made big contributions to our city's progress on diversity.

then riding the commuter train to Chicago. This resulted in long days for Lonnie and led to his introduction to Janesville racism in the police department of the early 2000s.

Lonnie would leave home in the dark to begin his commute to Chicago. On at least two occasions, he was stopped by a police officer, and when he asked why was told he had a taillight violation. Lonnie said he told the officer that his taillights were fine because it was a new car. He was let go that time and again another time when he was stopped and given the same explanation. His problem wasn't his taillights. He was certain he was stopped because he was a black man driving in Janesville in the dark early morning hours. He also experienced police cars following him in these early morning hours, but not stopping him.

Lonnie described another experience when he was working on his home, and a police officer approached him, responding to a call from a neighbor who thought Lonnie was a burglar. Lonnie told the officer that it was his home. It was not resolved until the officer called Lonnie's wife on the phone, and she confirmed that Lonnie was her husband, and it was their home. Lonnie said that over time, the neighbor became friends with his wife and eventually him. The neighbor, of course, was white as is Lonnie's wife.

The commute to Chicago meant he was up at 4 a.m. and back home between 7 and 8 p.m. So Lonnie applied for a job with several Janesville law firms. Several firms told him he was not a good fit.

He remembers being at the Country Kitchen in Janesville and "just not being waited on." He said he accepted it and left. He worked at several places in Janesville but was told to "stay in your lane," which he figured meant not to seek a promotion.

Lonnie's time in Janesville gradually got better. Police Chief Dave Moore began to make changes through education programs for his department. Lonnie has emerged as a strong, positive partner in his efforts to improve race relations in Janesville.

Lonnie serves on the African American Liaison Advisory Committee created by Chief Moore. He is also on the board of the Janesville Multicultural Teacher Scholarship Foundation, which provides scholarships to Janesville students of color who want to be teachers and then teach in Janesville.

Lonnie also serves on the Diversity Action Team, which I describe in Chapter 15, and on the committee that interviews police department applicants and makes recommendations to the police chief and the city's Police and Fire Commission. His day job is the director of Community Relations for the Boys and Girls Club of Janesville. He told me he now has five area police chiefs on speed dial, and they take his calls and he takes theirs. What a long journey from feeling racially profiled while just trying to drive to work!

There are now Town Hall meetings where police and citizens can express their opinions. Janesville also has 3-on-3 basketball games that pit Janesville kids against Janesville police officers. Brigham wants to bring Chicago artists to Janesville for Black History Month. He also told me he wants to be the face of diversity in Janesville.

Brigham told me that one of the greatest honors of his life came on May 15, 2018, when Chief Moore invited him to be the keynote speaker at the annual Police Memorial Program.

Chief Moore's reaching out to Lonnie was in keeping with the chief's philosophy—build trust; bring systemic change to the department; include everyone, not just the officers; and connect the passion to the mission. The chief has a very positive relationship with Lonnie and never hesitates to call him if he needs help or advice on various matters.

Chief Moore has brought in national experts to speak to the department on topics including the honor of policing, policy-oriented policing, implicit bias, and microaggressions. The chief has initiated a Latino Liaison Advisory Committee and Small Neighborhood Group Outings. These group outings occur in areas of Janesville where many residents lack trust in authority, including police. Hot dogs and a casual atmosphere, with about twelve police officers and the neighbors, gives everyone a chance to engage in individual conversations, which hopefully lead to the police and citizens having a better understanding of each other. Chief Moore's tireless work has led to a modern, better-informed police department to serve a racially diverse community.

There is still more to be done. The efforts of Chief Moore are impressive . He has one more effort to work on. There needs to be more diversity in the police force. There are four Hispanic officers. There are no black officers.

Sometimes fate brings two people with different backgrounds together at a critical time to work on a big problem. That is what happened when the white, lifelong Janesville resident Police Chief Dave Moore joined together with the black, Chicago-raised and Janesville resident Lonnie Brigham, Jr. to work to significantly improve relations between police and the Janesville citizens of color and then by extension improve race relations for everyone. We can't close the chapters in our past until we acknowledge that past.

I want to make it clear that while I have told some hard truths from Janesville's history— and the GM plant clearly mirrored that history—the people of America have no business looking askance at Janesville and its past. We all need to acknowledge that there are many communities in the United States whose story of a racist history and progress now gives hope, in the manner of the positive change in Janesville.

It's true, too, that going back to the 1850s and 1860s, Janesville has a proud history of support for ending slavery. It centered on the abolitionist movement and William Tallman, famous today because of the Lincoln-Tallman museum in Janesville, named such because Abraham Lincoln, while campaigning for the 1860 presidential nomination, was a guest of the Tallmans for two nights in 1859. Tallman was an active abolitionist, and he had found a candidate he could support.

Tallman also supported and hosted a reception for Frederick Douglass (1818–1895) who was an abolitionist, orator, and statesman. He escaped from slavery in Maryland and became a national leader in the abolition movement in Massachusetts and New York. He became known for his oratory and incisive writings. The abolitionist movement sought to end slavery before and during the Civil War.

One of his most famous quotes is, "Power concedes nothing without a demand. It never has and it never will."

Douglass advised presidents and gave lectures to thousands on a range of issues besides abolition including women's rights and Irish Home Rule. He has been called the father of the civil rights movement. He lectured across the north that the Civil War was about freeing the slaves.

Douglass came to Janesville to speak and was met at the railroad station by William Tallman, and then Tallman had a reception for him. The Rock County Historical Society provided me with this information, and my good friend Google helped as well.

Tallman was a leading or the leading abolitionist in Janesville. Greeting and treating this great African American Leader as an equal was a powerful message in Janesville in the 1850s and '60s. Tallman also showed his strong abolitionist views when in 1856 he bought arms and ammunition to help the anti-slavery side in the battles known to history as Bloody Kansas.

Tallman came to Janesville from New York State in 1849 and was a major land speculator in Rock and Green Counties. He died in 1878.His beautiful home is now the museum. ▌▌

13

Facing the Future: The Fate of Assembly Line Jobs, High Wages for Unskilled Labor, and Unions

I cannot write a book about the auto industry and not talk about the concept of the assembly line and its future. Henry Ford was given credit for creating the assembly line. He did it to allow Ford Motor Company to produce automobiles more efficiently (meaning less cost). The assembly line did that. Ford also said he wanted to produce a car at a cost that would allow the assembly line worker who built it to afford to buy it. That eventually worked, although the UAW helped this happen, not Henry Ford, by negotiating higher wages and benefits.

You may think I have a mixed opinion of Henry Ford after reading the paragraph above. I don't. He hired goons to beat up people, including Walter Reuther, who were trying to form unions. He also famously said about workers and the monotony of the assembly line, "Most workers do not want to think." That sounds like the opinion of an elitist and not based on any facts.

However, the workers on the assembly line paid a price that is impossible to assign a dollar amount. Put simply, the jobs were created to be monotonous! I experienced this in 1962 when I worked my first summer at the GM plant. I worked on the fourth trim line, and my job was simple (as were many of the jobs). My job was to bolt in the driver's side seat belts—that was it—about 60 times an hour for eight hours a day, five or six days a week.

I was paid well, earning $3.25 per hour at a time when most summer jobs outside GM paid between $1.00 and $1.50 per hour. To put this wage in perspective, both Cokes and tap beers cost 10 cents, and 12 oz. beers cost 25 cents in most taverns. (I, of course, learned this information from others!) McDonald's hamburgers were 15 cents. Tuition for one semester at Whitewater State University (now UW–Whitewater) was $110! That was one week's pay! Today one semester costs about $3,700.

This job was a great deal for me. It paid my way through college. I knew it was only for three months, not 30 years, and then I would be off to college until the next summer.

What about the worker who does this as a full-time job? Bolt in the driver's side seat belt for eight hours a day, 60 cars an hour, for at least 40 hours a week for at least 30 years. Good pay, good benefits, good for GM's profits, good for the family, but how do you feel as a person? The assembly line made good, smart people into human robots for eight hours a day.

"Work your way up the line." This means to not only work on the vehicle at your workstation but to move up the line and work on a few more vehicles, thus giving yourself about a five-minute break. This did not get a worker in trouble as long as it did not interfere with the other people working on the vehicle at their workstation. However, excessive "working up the line" could get a "time and motion study" on your job to see if a worker could handle more work (more tasks per vehicle). Workers would have a book, magazine, or newspaper to read a little bit during this few-minute break. So much for Henry Ford thinking the workers didn't want to think.

Janesville auto workers earned a minimum of $28 per hour at the time the plant closed in December 2008. It is well known in Janesville that some people thought the GM workers had it too good—that their pay was too high. I believe that at its core, this attitude was rooted in jealousy more than anything. I also think a significant majority of the city rejected this view.

I believe that the nature of assembly line work must be a factor in a discussion of the pay levels at GM. Yes, being represented by the UAW certainly helped and impacted the pay level, but assembly line work is boring as it was intended to be.

One can find thousands of GM workers who will tell you they stayed at GM for the pay and benefits despite the boring, non-challenging nature of assembly line work. Putting "bolt 42" in each vehicle for eight or more hours per day is in no way stimulating or rewarding. They did it to support their family, and that pay level afforded their family a middle-class lifestyle. That middle-class lifestyle had many positive consequences for the workers' children. It allowed tens of thousands of GM workers' children to attend post-high school education. Those students were able to say, "I was the first person in my family to go to college." I was one of those auto workers' children who has been able to say that.

GM paid for boredom. I believe there was a "boredom factor" built into the pay level. If the $28 per hour pay level in 2008 had been $18 per hour, I believe many good workers would have taken other jobs outside of GM for $18 or less per hour where they would have been challenged and offered a level of individual satisfaction for a job well done.

Henry Ford was given credit for developing the concept of the auto assembly line. I believe, however, that the concept of the assembly line where each worker did one "piece" of the work that combined with a thousand or several thousand other workers each doing their one "piece" had consequences that should be acknowledged.

Monotony does not explain the difference between $18 and $28 per hour. GM did not pay another $10 as a "boredom" cost. But I do believe they did pay some people more for boredom to keep and attract good workers.

There was another reason to stay in those jobs and build up seniority. There were other coveted jobs off the assembly line filled with people with the most seniority. So if you stayed long enough, you would likely get one of those jobs that involved less tedious tasks off the assembly line that required thinking.

It's a hard, cold reality that most assembly line jobs can be replaced with a robot. This is the future of assembly line jobs across America in the auto industry and other industries. Robots need a certain number of workers to maintain them, but not very many.

This begs the question. What is the future of jobs for young people who do not seek some post-high school education to learn specialized skills? For most, it will mean jobs at modest wages, which often leads to the need for a second job. These folks work hard to support their families. They spend long hours at work resulting in less time for cooking good food, playing with the kids, overseeing homework, and getting them to bed on time, etc. America has faced economic changes before and will again.

The positive news is that there will be new jobs in new industries with new products. Think of all the inventions that have created new jobs in American history: radio, electricity, typewriter, automobile, airplane, telephone, computer, etc. Each invention created millions of new jobs. The catch is that new jobs will almost surely require education beyond high school, and it likely means lifetime learning as change becomes more rapid with new technologies and more education.

I suspect the Foxconn factory to be built in Racine County will be filled with robots and fewer humans. Time will prove me right or wrong.

In 2019, I see wages at about $16 an hour, at the top end, for unskilled jobs. What does $16 per hour mean in 2019? Working 40 hours per week means annual earnings of about $32,000 per year. This almost always means no pension and maybe some level of health insurance but not the insurance coverage that gives parents confidence their family would be protected against unexpected sickness.

It also means the need for two or more jobs for a single parent or family with two parents. That means parents are not home for much of their children's after-school time. As I noted above, that is less time to make sure homework is done and that kids get to bed on time. There's less time to cook healthy meals, so fast food must do.

When unskilled workers must work 60 hours per week or more and try to make time for their family and to sleep, do they have time to attend college or technical school? America's political elite have a simple solution: If you are unskilled, go back to school and learn a skill. This would be doable if we had 32-hour days.

Unions may have once been the answer, but Janesville and Rock County saw a dramatic decrease in the number of people who belonged to either a public or private sector union, from 24,000 in 2006 to 4,000 in 2016 (*Janesville Gazette*, 9/3/17). This dramatic drop was largely related to two events: GM closing in 2008 and the passage of Act 10 by the state, which took away almost all bargaining rights from public sector unions. Rock County is a microcosm of union membership nationally, though the decline nationwide since 2000 has not been nearly as drastic as in Rock County. It is necessary to point out that a big part of this reduction (no public data available), besides the closing of GM, is the number of public employees; teachers; and county, state, and city employees who still have their jobs but have stopped paying union dues because their union now has so little power they have decided it's not worth paying them. There is some statewide data that the membership in AFSCME (city and county employees) and WEAC (teachers) has shrunk by 60 percent or more. These declines in membership are only known by the public when the unions choose to release them. This is the story of the last 10 years in Janesville. The future is unknown, but the following is a brief description of the conditions that led to the success of unionization.

The post-Civil War industrial boom in the United States resulted in workers, mostly in factories, mines, and other locations, having no collective power. Their working conditions were frequently awful, unsafe, low paying, with no benefits, long hours six or seven days per week. There were no child labor laws, no worker compensation laws, no unemployment compensation programs, and workers faced losing their jobs at management's discretion.

All the above working conditions led to workers choosing unions. Unions at the negotiating table and political support (sometimes from both political parties) greatly improved working conditions beginning in the 1930s.

So, what is the future?

First, we must acknowledge that technology and the workplace itself have led to a different workplace, and the need for large numbers of workers in large manufacturing buildings has shrunk. Computers allow people to do a job from anywhere, and robots are replacing people on assembly lines.

I mention these changes in the workplace because it has historically been easier to increase union members in large numbers by organizing at a large plant or office.

What do we know about the future of jobs in America, or what can we reasonably speculate?

• We cannot name the 10 largest employers 40 years from now or 20 years from now. Perhaps we'll have an explosion of small employers and self-employed people.

• Small or nonexistent business today may be huge businesses in America 20 years from now. Think of Amazon, Netflix, Apple, Google, etc. today compared to their size or existence just 20 years ago.

• Driverless and electric vehicles are seemingly inevitable. What does this mean for truck drivers (teamsters), cab drivers in unions, gas stations, and the convenience stores so frequently attached to them?

- I assume that every piece of technology we use today has people around the world working on better technology. The robot of today may be an antique in the next several years.

- I don't know what all the above mean for unions. We can speculate that unions will be recruiting members who work in yet to be created businesses doing yet to be created jobs.

I think it is possible that any resurgence of unions in the private sector may have as much to do with the behavior of management as it does with union organizing efforts. If management treats their employees fairly with reasonable pay increases and benefits, union organizing will be difficult. If they abuse their power, union organizing will be more successful.

The future of public sector unions in Wisconsin and any other state will depend on politics and elections. I believe the millennial generation is a wildcard in this matter. My read on many of them is that they are not particularly pro-union, but they do believe in treating employees fairly. As they come to positions of power and retain this view, that could make union organizing more difficult in companies led by CEOs with this progressive view. In my first book I talked about the millennial generation and called them "the most tolerant generation" of other people's skin color, religious views, political views, etc.

Tom Brokaw has called the Depression/World War II generation "the greatest generation." I certainly do not dispute this description. However, with all the change and the pace of change coming to America's economy and job availability and how different it will be from the past 100 years, there is a chance that if millennials perform as I believe they will, they may at least tie as the greatest generation. Time will tell what happens. ▮▮

14
Janesville Without GM

There was considerable "trickle down" pain to Janesville due to the loss of GM and its supplier companies at the end of 2008.

The GM plant built the last SUV on December 23, 2008. The plant was idled completely on April 23, 2009, after building the last Isuzu. This was a separate small project in a different area, and this led to the layoffs of GM's last 57 workers. Four thousand five hundred good- paying jobs were lost between GM and at the area supplier plants. There is no accurate data of other jobs lost or hours reduced by the impact of this event (on workers in retail stores, hairdressers, auto salespeople, bartenders, bowling alley staff, realtors, etc.).

Janesville lost 3,000 UAW jobs during 2008 (of the 4,500) and about 250 management and other non-union jobs that paid a minimum of $28 per hour plus benefits. Some, of course, were people who lived within 30 miles of Janesville (and often shopped in Janesville). This occurred as Janesville was also experiencing the national recession. It was a devastating blow for Janesville.

Amy Goldstein does a good job of reporting the impact on families directly affected by the GM closing in her excellent book *Janesville: An American Story*. She follows families representative of different impacts precipitated by the loss of a family member's job at GM.

I have no need to duplicate her efforts. I do, however, want to report the enormous and often unnoticed impact the closing had on every retail business. If your business involved selling anything to Janesville citizens, you were hurt—the only question is how deeply. Retail business workers saw a decrease in hours worked or the elimination of their jobs because of a decrease in sales, and it certainly hurt the bottom line of businesses. Here are some examples:

- Bowling alleys saw significant drops in the number of teams in their leagues. Not bowling in the once-a-week leagues saved families $20 to $30 per week. One of the biggest bowling alleys in Janesville, Blackbridge Bowl, saw big reductions in their leagues and closed in 2016.

- Hair salons saw a significant change in the frequency of women making appointments. For example, rather than going once every one to two weeks, people would go once every four to six weeks. Salons saw a big loss of business in manicures. Kevin Hein, who has cut my hair for 35 years, told me their nail business was hurt even more than their hair business. This, of course, led to fewer appointments, fewer tips, and fewer hours of work. This was significantly related to the GM closing. There is no other way to explain the timing of this loss of business. These changes started in 2009. Kevin also noticed that many customers who worked at the supplier plants that closed moved to other cities for work, and that reduced the number of customers.

- Taverns that served lunch and dinner saw something new after GM closed. It was, of course, not unusual to have customers pay for lunches and evening meals with a credit card. People started ordering two beers and paying for the five dollar tab with their credit card. Tavern owners concluded that people were using their credit cards to attempt to maintain their lifestyle from before GM closed.

- Retailers in the Janesville Mall also told me anecdotal stories of lower sales after GM closed.

- Realtors, whose business was already hurt by the housing bubble burst of 2006, saw home sales drop after GM closed. There were many people interested in selling their homes, but there were few buyers.

- The great years of GM in Janesville meant that many of those thousands of employees would buy a new car every two or three years. The year 2008 changed that. It became more common to make that new vehicle last four, five, or more years, resulting in fewer new and used car sales, fewer salespeople or at least fewer hours, and less income for those who still had jobs in that business.

- Poverty levels increased. Students eligible for free and reduced lunches jumped from 33 percent in the early 2000s to 50 percent within two years of the plant closing. The free and reduced lunch number is the most commonly used measurement of poverty in a community. Certain areas of Janesville were even harder hit. Three elementary schools had free and reduced lunch percentages above 70 percent, and one of those was above 90 percent. At another school it was only 29 percent.

- Several schools opened "closets" where generous teachers and members of the community donated money, clothing, food, and personal items that were given to students who individually or with their family needed these necessities of life. There was no tax money used in connection with these closets (rooms in the schools). The closets represent Janesville at its best, and the need for these closets tells the "under the radar" human damage when you add the GM loss to the simultaneous national recession. These closets are still open and still needed in 2019.

- Another way to look at the income impact that GM's closing had on the Janesville community is to compare GM/UAW contributions to the United Way campaign before the plant closed and after thousands lost their jobs. The GM/UAW joint effort had been a significant contribution to the United Way, as shown in the following table:

Year	GM/UAW Contribution	United Way Total
2003	$417,072	$1,771,715
2004	$425,856	$1,826,310
2007	$351,722	$1,671,699
2008	$88,473	$1,283,088
2009	$39,564	$1,343,935

In the good years (2003 and 2004), GM/UAW contributed about 25 percent of all the money given to the United Way. Production started to slow down in 2007, and the GM/UAW number was lower. Then in 2008 GM announced that the plant would close, and the contribution shrunk considerably, and you can see its impact on the total raised by the United Way. The GM/UAW number then shrunk drastically in 2009 with the plant closure.

It should be mentioned that historically leadership of the United Way was made up of business leaders in the community. However, Ron Monat, a longtime member of the United Way board, became the first and only union leader to be chosen as both the annual fundraising campaign chairman and as president of the United Way board. He also served on the Janesville Police and Fire Commission.

In her book *On Death and Dying*, Elisabeth Kübler-Ross described five stages of grief: denial, anger, bargaining, depression, and acceptance. For many decades, GM was a significant part of Janesville's identity, and that loss was felt both individually and as a community. While the loss of a company and the jobs it takes with it is not the same as the loss of a loved one, I do believe that there is some similarity in the recovery process. The citizenry goes through some of these stages or other related emotions and needs time to accept the new economic reality it faces. Cities need to acknowledge some level of this cycle, and time for it must be factored into their recovery strategy. Many Janesville citizens, and others up to 40 miles away, who were affected went through these feelings. Getting through that range of feelings and emotions cannot be rushed.

Janesville was not going to recover quickly. "Cheerleading" for Janesville was necessary, but this pain for so many was real. The only way to have avoided this pain would have been the 100 to 1 shot that GM reopened or a great-paying replacement for GM came to town. Neither happened.

Janesville did have a great number of things going for it. Janesville had not lost its excellent infrastructure just because

GM was gone. The following, in no particular order, gave us hope:

- Excellent railroad connections
- An interstate highway in close proximity to Janesville
- An airport
- A solid public education system including a two-year University of Wisconsin campus and a technical school
- Clean, honest local government
- A beautiful river running through the city that is now supporting economic growth
- A widely recognized good work ethic
- Health care competition (Mercy Health Care System and Dean-St. Mary's)
- 2,500 UAW retirees with pensions
- Janesville, sitting on I-90, is also a commuter town. Two much larger communities, Madison, Wisconsin, and Rockford, Illinois, are within one hour's driving distance as well as many other communities within 45 minutes. People can work in those communities and spend their paycheck in Janesville. This is a common occurrence in two worker households where one works in Janesville and the other in one of the other cities. Or both work somewhere else.

The year 2019 finds Janesville continuing its comeback. It was always going to be slower than we wanted. Our downtown is being revitalized with special use of the Rock River. There are serious efforts to develop a "post GM economy." This is not an easy or quick process.

I believe that after ten years, Janesville is at the fifth stage of grief: acceptance. It took quite a while, and the selling of the plant in 2017 and its demolition in 2018 and 2019 contributed to the acceptance. (Acceptance, however, is not the same as forgetting our GM past. That may take 50 years or more.) Later I'll describe specific projects that have been announced between 2017 and 2019 or are already being implemented.

It should be noted that the longshot hope that the GM plant's standby status would lead to their return was held while not realizing that if they did come back, the wages would not have been like they were in 2008.

The GM-UAW contract that was finalized in August 2008 had a brand-new item: a two-tiered pay schedule. All existing employees would continue to earn at least $28 per hour. But new employees would have a starting wage of $14.85 per hour (a number that would increase with each new four-year contract, and it has, and now 10 years later it is about $18 per hour). Though good, the $30 plus minimum that those employed in 2008 would be earning was now gone for all new employees.

Had GM returned after a few years, most of the employees would be new hires at the lower wage. The 2008 employees that went to other plants could not return to Janesville for two years, and those who retired and took buyouts would need to apply for employment, and if hired, would earn the new lower wage. All new employees would earn $14.85 per hour or its equivalent as the years went on. And over time, everyone would be a new employee. Another factor to consider is that with each passing year, it would be possible that more robots would replace workers.

Let me be clear. Janesville would have been ecstatic if GM had returned. But the old, great hourly wage was history. However, $15 to $18 per hour depending on what year they returned, plus health insurance and a pension would have been good news for thousands of families and the community. This would have been the wage for well over half the employees. The pension and health insurance would have made these jobs the most attractive in that wage range. They would also have a union to fight for higher wages in future years.

The real obstacle to GM ever returning to Janesville was GM's overcapacity problem. They closed Janesville and three other plants in 2008, but they also closed 12 plants in 2007 and 12 plants in 2009.

While I noted above many things Janesville still has going for it today, I should mention new data in a story in the *Janesville Gazette* on August 28, 2018, that told of a disturbing report on the current status and trends on poverty levels and the working poor in Janesville and Rock County. The headline of the story is "Report: Rock County's 'working poor' population is growing."

Middle- and upper-income Janesville is doing well, but those in lower incomes and poverty have not improved their financial condition between 2010 and 2016 (dates of the latest data). Anecdotal evidence from the United Way's Helpline indicates this data has not improved as of 2018.

The data is from the ALICE Project, a national report the United Way releases every two years. I believe that a majority of people, including me, consider the United Way a credible organization without a political philosophy bent to the political left or right. ALICE (Asset Limited, Income Constrained, Employed) represents financially struggling households, even though they have jobs.

Thirty-one percent of Rock County households are in this category, plus another 11 percent are in the federal poverty category. This means that 42 percent of Rock County households were poor or the working poor in 2016. It was 37 percent in 2010.

Mary Fanning-Penny, the president of Rock County's United Way, said in the article that data shows that in Rock County 60 percent of households earn less than $20 per hour. That counts all household income, meaning it could include more than one job.

I realize this is countywide data, but as I point out in a different chapter, the workforce at the GM plant who lived in Janesville varied between 50 percent and 60 percent. So then 40 percent to 50 percent lived mostly in the rest of Rock County with a small percent living outside Rock County but within driving distance. The plant closing hurt the whole county, so I believe using this countywide data is telling in the story of our difficult recovery from the closing of the plant, the drastic reduction in union jobs in Rock County, and the new jobs paying much less than GM. That's why though the unemployment rate is low, near 4 percent, it does not tell the real story of the economic status of the majority of households in Rock County.

Political officeholders love to brag about the low unemployment rate (like they deserve credit for it), but the per hour wage tells the real story.

A 2018 study by the Center on Wisconsin Strategy (COWS) found that across all of Wisconsin, one in every five workers is earning under the poverty level ($11.95 per hour). This group of workers totals 675,000 citizens. This statewide data is similar to the "two Janesville" data discussed above.

It is easy to say that there are today "two Janesvilles" and explain it beyond the generality of the well-off and those with low income despite having two jobs. That is true, but most people want it quantified.

My best numerical example of this is that there is an elementary school on the east side of Janesville where only 29 percent of the students have household incomes low enough to qualify for free lunch. There is another elementary school on the south side of the city where over 90 percent of the students are eligible for the free lunch program. To qualify for reduced or free lunch, a family of four must have a household income of $39,000 or less.

This is what I mean by two Janesvilles. It seems essential to me that we remember there are both. The goal should not be to try and downplay the existence of poverty, but rather that those with the means to help have a goal to reduce and hopefully eliminate poverty.

The COWS study also looked at union membership in public and private sector jobs and found significant drops in union membership.

Overall, 24 percent of the state's workers were union members in the early 1980s, and now the total is 8.3 percent. The study said Act 10 and right-to-work law changes were largely responsible for the decline. Unions have always meant higher wages for workers in similar jobs.

If Janesville has struggled since the plant closing, it seems fair to say General Motors has, too. The company went through bankruptcy in 2009. This was an event that even one year earlier would have been impossible to believe for most Americans, including almost everyone in Janesville. According to author Steven Rattner, the leadership of GM wouldn't consider it even into early 2009.

Well, it happened. Rattner describes it in *Overhaul*. He gives the following succinct description of how it would work:

> The bankruptcy plan envisioned for GM was an outsized version of the one designed for Chrysler. With the help of many billions of taxpayer dollars, GM would separate its assets into two companies. "Old GM" would retain the factories, equipment, brands, and real estate that the business no longer needed. Its sole purpose would be to dispose of these assets using the proceeds to repay the

creditors that the other company, Shiny New GM, had left behind. The new company would own all the assets GM did intend to keep free of crippling costs and debts. This new business would go forth as a streamlined, revitalized competitor on the world automotive scene. We meant it to be not only viable but also highly profitable.

There are numerous details involved in a bankruptcy involving billions of dollars. Lay people like me get lost in the terminology. I have learned two common language ways to describe the basic reality of bankruptcy.

The first is that a company going through bankruptcy stops paying its bills. Wouldn't all our financial situations get a lot better if we stopped making house payments, car payments, student loan payments?

The second way to describe bankruptcy is to view it as taking your car through a car wash. Think of the mud and dirt on your car as the company's debt. You go into the car wash with all this dirt (debt) and come out the other end all clean of dirt (debt).

What did this mean for the closed Janesville plant? From the above description of the "two" GMs post-bankruptcy, I would have assumed for sure Janesville would have been in the Motor Liquidation Company (MLC or old GM). But it wasn't. In May 2009, GM had designated three closed plants in Janesville; Spring Hill, Tennessee; and Orion Township in Michigan to be on standby status. This was intended, or so GM said, to provide more capacity if the new GM saw sales take off. Therefore, Janesville's longshot hope of GM reopening the plant was alive, but a very longshot (at least to me and many others in Janesville).

There was also another factor. The UAW had language in its contract with GM stating that GM could not sell the Janesville plant without the UAW signing off on it. This language stayed in the GM-UAW contracts (four-year contracts) until the contract was signed in 2015. GM then sold the plant in late 2017 without any sign they wanted or needed to reopen it. It is worth reporting that GM did reopen the other two standby plants.

It's interesting to note that in November 2018, General Motors CEO Mary Barra announced that GM would be reducing their workforce by about 15,000 employees in the U.S. and Canada. This total includes 8,000 white-collar workers and a smaller number of UAW workers. She also announced the likely closing of up to five plants in the U.S. and Canada. GM also said that its plants are operating at 70 percent capacity. She was, not surprisingly, met with severe criticism from President Trump and the UAW. Her reason for the reductions was that the cars being assembled in these plants aren't selling.

Guess what? Consumers have severely slowed down their desire to buy cars. They are choosing trucks, crossovers, and SUVs. According to GM, in October 2018, 65 percent of their new vehicle sales were trucks or SUVs. That is up from 50 percent in 2013. GM said they would stop production of several of their car models.

Barra was quoted saying, "GM does not foresee an economic downturn but is making the cuts to get in front of it while the company and the economy are strong."

The criticism of Barra reminds me (again) of what I said in my first book about government leaders who take preemptive actions that avoid bigger future problems. They never get credit. The public has not yet felt the pain of doing nothing. Leaders who help fix a problem after it occurs get credit. It turns out that this reality applies to business leaders, too.

I also find the immediate criticism of Barra ignores the blistering criticism of GM just 10 years ago when they went broke and went through bankruptcy in 2009. Rattner's book *Overhaul* is clear that GM went broke because GM's top management refused to make any tough decisions.

To avoid worsening problems, Barra is taking action by doing the exact things her predecessors refused to do in the years and decades before they tumbled into bankruptcy and were saved with a taxpayer loan of close to $60 billion. What can we learn from all of this? Read history, and in this case, recent history. Ten years is not that long ago.

Only time will tell the consequences of Barra's decisions. She made a decision knowing the criticism she would receive. We will never know what would have happened to GM if they had CEOs like Barra in the 1990s and 2000s.

With the selling of the plant in 2017, the Janesville-GM saga was finally over. GM was now gone. The standby status was, in my view, a tease. I could not find out who made that standby decision. Was it GM as a favor to the UAW? Was it Obama? Was it a demand of the UAW in the give and take of contract negotiations? I do know that it delayed Janesville's full acceptance of the reality that GM was gone and not coming back.

It can be said that the UAW International officials had some responsibility, as they wanted the "sign off" language in the contracts. This language allowed GM to leave the plant standing there and put off any possibility of having to pay any environmental clean-up costs, and they could blame the situation on the UAW. Leaving that old plant standing idle for 10 years did not make people in Janesville feel good. It delayed full acceptance that GM was gone for good.

Let me now briefly address the notion, expressed by some around Janesville, that the city is better off without GM. Their argument was that GM and high wages kept other companies from locating in Janesville because they would be forced to pay high wages to compete for workers with GM.

This was a classic case of a statement that could not be proven wrong while GM was here. This view also ignored the input the good wages at GM had on the workers' families for decades. It also ignores the contributions by management and UAW workers to the United Way—25 percent of all contributions for years when the plant was open. And the union donated generously to several charities. I believe that this view was also influenced by certain leaders who didn't like organized labor, and the UAW was an influential union. The UAW had also organized workers in other businesses, including the supplier plants to GM, health care facilities, and credit unions.

Now it is nearly eleven years since GM closed. So where are the companies that didn't come here because they didn't want to compete with GM wages and possibly have their employees form a union? I don't know where they are, but they're not in Janesville.

The eventual buyer of the Janesville plant and the property indicated shortly after finalizing the purchase that they would tear it down. They expressed much optimism at a press conference in Janesville in December 2017 that it is a wonderful piece of property with great train, interstate, airport, and utility access.

The buyer was Commercial Development Company (CDC), a St. Louis-based company. They have plenty of experience in buying buildings and properties such as the Janesville site, including other closed GM plants. Their general method of operation is to use a brief few months to determine if there is a buyer for the existing buildings and then tear them down if there is not a "quick" buyer. There was not one for the Janesville GM plant.

CDC held a public open house in Janesville on September 25, 2018, to provide the community with an update on their plan as of that date. They will now market the site. They indicate the two rail lines connected to the site plus easy access for trucks to I-90 (because of Reuther Way and the Avalon Road I-90 Interchange, explicitly built by the taxpayers to please GM). Could they now play an important role in the economic future of Janesville?

CDC does not operate businesses on sites like Janesville. They prepare and market the site. They were effusive with their belief that the railroad connection makes the site especially attractive. They mentioned the attractiveness of the site as a distribution center. This, of course, is not manufacturing, and their very large buildings usually do not need large numbers of employees. We now have a large Dollar General distribution center on the south side of Janesville near the Avalon Road Interchange. It provides jobs in the wage range of $14 to $18 per hour. This could well be the range of wages at a new distribution center.

CDC referred to the expected development as a railroad centric development. That could mean lots of products moving in and out of the site with none or almost none of it manufactured here.

Still, Janesville has survived. I'm proud of my city and want now to tell you why. ▮▮

15

Slow Recovery and Janesville's Good Heart

The process of tearing down the GM plant and Janesville's recovery is making progress. The last week of September 2018 brought a major announcement. The company that purchased the GM property revealed more details of their plans to make the GM site a railroad centric redevelopment site. They envision several separate parcels that could each support the development of new industries, including distribution centers.

CDC's redevelopment proposal shows seven new buildings ranging in size between 210,000 square feet and 538,000 square feet, plus two light industrial districts and about 15 small buildings on the north and south edges of the property. It is another big step toward Janesville moving on from its GM past.

CDC said they intend to rename the GM site Centennial Industrial Park as a tip of the cap to GM's 100 years of history in Janesville. Another salute to Janesville and GM history came with the May 17, 2019, announcement by Blackhawk Community Credit Union (BHCCU) of their finalized plans for a General Motors Legacy Center at the downtown site of the vacant Chase Bank on East Milwaukee Street, just one block from the Rock River and immediately adjacent to the Arise project. The building is in an excellent location for preserving Janesville's history as it sits directly next to the monument honoring the 99 heroes of World War II who endured the Bataan Death March and wound up POWs in Japan for more than three years. Next to that monument is another honoring the Janesville veterans of World War I.

The original plan was to construct a new building for BHCCU (that would have included the Legacy Center) on the Rock River on the south side of the downtown area. The new plan, putting the Legacy Center in the Chase Bank site, potentially increases the Legacy Center's space from 10,000 to 24,000 square feet. It will contain local GM memorabilia and give former GM families and the community a place to remember its past.

I believe there is a tremendous appetite for this Janesville-GM history. The city witnessed it in 2019 when the bricks from the wall that separated the Fisher Body Division and the Chevrolet Division in the original plant were given away. They had been saved, then cleaned by volunteers. An announcement let people know that on May 4 the bricks would be distributed. People lined up for over a mile in their vehicles. It was amazing and poignant. People came from other states. Over 3,000 bricks were given out, two bricks per vehicle. Legacy Center Director Dona Dutcher summed up the emotional connection of the people in the 1,500 or more vehicles when she said, "Every car has multiple stories in it." This book would likely be over 2,000 pages if I could write all those stories.

After I sat in line waiting for my turn to get two bricks, I spent about a half hour with the volunteers. They clearly knew they were part of an extraordinary day. The enormous turnout sent a clear message that the impact of the GM plant still runs deep in thousands of families in Janesville and beyond.

Before moving on from the Legacy Center and BHCCU, I want to share how much the credit union's existence meant to my dad, who was a UAW member in 1964 when Local 95 started a credit union for their members in a building on Academy Street. It evolved into BHCCU. I was a 20-year-old college kid then, and I remember clearly how happy my dad was that he could do his banking business with people he related to and trusted. No longer did he have to have his car loan and home loan at a bank where he felt no connection or relationship with its leadership. I do not doubt that other UAW members shared my dad's feelings. This BHCCU/Legacy Center connection feels good.

I briefly mentioned earlier the public-private project called Arise. It continues to grow and expand in downtown Janesville with many of their projects centering around the Rock River. Their goal is to attract people to downtown Janesville by making it a center of activity including shopping, dining, festivals, and performances at the outdoor stages or the nearby Janesville Performing Arts Center, and a place to sit or walk around and enjoy the beauty of the Rock River.

The recovery continues. However, in early 2019 Janesville is still missing new medium or large manufacturers, or even a few medium-sized employers, though we have benefited from the construction and opening of St. Mary's Hospital.

Along with recognizing these seeds of economic rebirth, I want to note that while I have written in this book about racism in Janesville and GM from the 1950s through the 1970s, and some of the city's other problems as well, Janesville is a much better place today. A great example of this is the generosity of its citizens. We have a strong United Way and so much more to offer. Rock County is the home to approximately 1,500 nonprofit organizations!

We have a big food pantry and more through a church-based organization called Everyone Cooperating to Help Others (ECHO). ECHO is best known for its food pantry, but with the help of grants and the generosity of citizens, they also do a considerable amount of work with rental assistance and rapid rehousing. They are starting a transitional housing program, partnering with the City of Janesville's Community Development Authority to acquire a single-family home for families to regain stability and move on to permanent housing within 24 months.

We have Health Net, a free health clinic for low-income people staffed by volunteer doctors, dentists, and nurses. Private contributions fund the overhead costs.

Gifts Men's Shelter began in 2007 with six churches rotating overnight staffing for homeless men. Today nearly 40 churches support the organization, which now has a permanent shelter, case management, education, food, and clothing. The shelter also runs Life Recovery Home, a transitional place between the shelter and permanent housing.

The YWCA Shelter for Battered Women first opened in 1980, and a new shelter opened in its current location in 2001. Other services in transitional living through the YWCA are CARE House for forensic interviews of abused children, Immigration Outreach services, and childcare programming.

The Red Road House is a substance abuse recovery program that is currently working to become a state certified community-based residential facility (CBRF). Billy Bob Grahn is a recovering substance abuser who provides a caring place to help those who wish to work toward recovery. He is a member of the Bad River Band of the Lake Superior Chippewa. I like him a great deal.

The Homeless Intervention Task Force was started 20 years ago to create a countywide continuum of care and to be a coalition of programs working together to receive state grant funding for homelessness. Recently, Janesville's city manager has also created a separate homeless task force to find solutions to the city's growing homeless population. Solutions are in the works, but there has not yet been any formalized new programming.

The Janesville Police Department (JPD) created the African American Liaison Advisory Committee (AALAC) and the Latino Liaison Advisory Committee (LLAC) to help the JPD build trust and understanding with those populations.

Closets exist in both high schools, in two middle schools, and several of the elementary schools. These rooms provide basic needs for low-income students including clothing, food, personal items, and more. This program has no taxpayer costs. Private citizen contributions pay for everything, and teachers and retired teachers volunteer their time to staff the closets.

Meals on Wheels is a program of volunteers from about 20 churches that deliver hot meals to elderly and disabled citizens who do not have the physical ability, transportation, or money to go out for lunch.

Bags of Hope is a Christmastime program run by the School District of Janesville since 2009. They took over the program from the UAW which started and ran the program until the plant closed and UAW membership and resources shrunk substantially. The program provides two weeks of groceries for nearly 400 low-income families in Janesville. Generosity from local businesses and donations from hundreds of citizens fund this program. Hundreds of volunteers fill the grocery bags with meat, vegetables, eggs, a sack of potatoes, toilet tissue, and a lot more, and about 100 vehicles of volunteers deliver the items just before Christmas. My friend Doug Heenan and I deliver every year, and the gratitude and warmth of the people who receive this food are incredibly touching. I only wish more people could experience this reaction. The Salvation Army also plays an active role in providing meals and a range of resources.

The Janesville Multicultural Teacher Scholarship (JMTS) is a private contribution funded scholarship that awards up to $5,000 yearly to Janesville students of color who are going to college to get teaching degrees and agree to teach in Janesville upon graduation. This program is intended to have the teachers mirror the diverse student population. The students are currently much more racially diverse than their teachers. I started the foundation in 2008. All profits from this book go to this foundation.

The Diversity Action Team (DAT) is a racially diverse group of Janesville citizens who spread the message of the strength of racial diversity and what it can bring to Janesville.

There are also a large number of Janesville residents who belong to no group, never seek or get public acknowledgment of their good deeds, but nevertheless, visit the sick, take friends or strangers to doctor appointments, coach young people in a variety of youth sports, or work with young people who are growing up without the adult guidance they need. Many people volunteer in our elementary schools and read to students or listen to students read.

These programs don't care about the skin color of the people they serve, and the people being helped do not care about the skin color of the people who are helping them. Today Janesville is a wonderful place to live and raise a family. **ıl**

16

What Janesville Can Teach America

I asked the question in a previous chapter about how much control GM management in Janesville and UAW Local 95 had over their destiny. Unions and management fought terrible fights over what each wanted when their fate was overwhelmingly determined by issues and events that were out of their control.

This leads me to ask a larger question: to what extent was the City of Janesville in control of its destiny regarding the closing of GM? As a result of the events that unfolded in Janesville, other cities can learn and understand that a city and its people can experience unforeseen circumstances beyond their control.

How could Janesville know that GM was going broke? How can a community really know the financial situation of its largest employers? I have some advice for those cities based on the Janesville experience.

1. The community needs to recognize and acknowledge that the future of the large company in your community is not up to the community. The city is almost totally at the mercy of the company unless you happen to be lucky enough to have a powerful politician in Washington, and there are not many of those. Janesville had Les Aspin, but his real power only lasted from 1985 to 1994.

Cities of all sizes across America are in the situation that Janesville experienced—one large employer who is owned by a corporation located out of state. It isn't always a manufacturer. It could be a large insurance company or another industry.

2. Diversify your economy. When a community is over-reliant on one employer, that company "owns" the community, meaning there is little power or control over that employer's future in the community. Diversification is obvious but not easy to do, and often it is put off when times are good with the big employer. Diversification in Janesville was never a public priority, at least since 1970.

3. Be concerned if your city's largest employer's corporate headquarters is not in your state. The corporation will have more relationships in the corporation's home state than in yours. This could matter if that corporation is ever deciding between your community and one in their home state. GM moved some of the Janesville workload, the medium-duty truck, to GM's home state of Michigan in 2004. GM also chose Michigan over Janesville when they were deciding where to put production of the Chevy Spark in 2009.

4. Be even more concerned if your city is the only location in your state for a large out-of-state corporation. That

corporation, if faced with the need to close a plant, will have a strong inclination to close the plant in the state where they have no other plants. They will not be concerned with unhappy politicians in that state, as they will no longer have any presence there. Janesville was GM's only assembly plant in Wisconsin.

5. That large company that plays a dominant role in the economy of your community is owned by a corporation that very often is located out of state. You will find as we discovered in Janesville that there are two managements: The local management team and the management team at corporate headquarters. They are all part of one corporate structure for sure, but they have different concerns, goals, and hopes. Whether your local company stays, goes, expands, or shrinks will be decided by corporate headquarters, not the local management team.

Local employees and local management can use their shared goal of keeping the company in town and hopefully expanding the workload. Therefore, the often historic lack of cooperation between labor (union or nonunion) and management at the local level should stop, and both parties recognize that more unites them than divides them. It's obvious that if your plant closes, everyone loses their job.

Janesville labor and management realized this in 1986, and their cooperation played a significant role in the plant staying open for 22 more years.

6. Don't be used. If a corporation wants to leave your community, offering them taxpayer-paid financial incentives can only work if they are genuinely undecided on leaving and the tax money tilts them toward staying. A corporation would like to have two or more communities competing for the jobs. This results in one state's taxpayers competing against another

state's taxpayers and is often influenced by the willingness of a state's politicians to commit their taxpayers' money so the politician looks good. A politician does not want their community or state to lose jobs. But it would also be naive not to acknowledge that they deeply fear being blamed for the loss. The loss is bad. Being blamed for it is a big problem for their career. This competition is often used by the corporation to get more money out of their favored site by telling them to put in a best and final offer (BAFO) that is more money than another state's bid.

I firmly believe that this happened in 2008 in our attempts to keep the GM plant in Janesville. I doubt GM will ever confirm this unless some former GM executive "finds religion" and decides to speak out about it.

While the GM Retention Task Force was putting together our financial package, we had two conference calls with Detroit GM management. The calls were helpful to us: asking questions and hearing Detroit give us some direction on what they wanted in the financial package. Detroit made very clear they did not want tax credits spread out over 10 to 20 years.

A large part of our package would be state tax credits (about 75 percent of the package). A big issue with tax credits is over how many years they are spread. For example, $100 million in tax credits spread out over 20 years are not as valuable as $100 million over just five years. It is also easier for a governor to offer credits (our tax money) spread out over many years for two reasons: you can offer a bigger number, and the cost down the line will be a future governor's problem.

We listened to Detroit's advice, and our $160 million in tax credits were to be paid out in five years. Our total package was over $200 million. Michigan offered a much bigger number, but their tax credits were spread out over more than 10 years. This competition was for the production of the fuel-efficient Chevy Spark, which would replace the SUV production we were losing in 2008. We were never given a chance to submit a best and final offer (BAFO) to beat Michigan. Michigan won. We were not supposed to win.

7. Much of the human pain over the loss of jobs is felt in lower-income families, and too much of it is unseen and unfelt by many others in the community. Public attention has historically focused on the unemployment rate to assess the strength of the economy. I believe this is overrated as a measurement of whether the economy of a community is getting better in the 21st century. Why? If a person loses a $28 per hour job and the best job they can get is $12 to $16 per hour, the unemployment rate has not changed but multiplied over thousands of workers, and household incomes have severely shrunk.

I believe it more instructive and telling to look at the number of students in the local public schools who are eligible for free lunches because of low household income. Janesville students eligible for free lunches rose rapidly after the 2008 plant closing and has not moderated a decade later.

The School District of Janesville student population between 2009 and 2018 was relatively flat. The 2009–2010 student population was 9,772, and in 2017–2018 it was 9,735. The number of students eligible for the free school lunches rose from 3,295 in the 2007–2008 school year to 4,543 in the 2017–2018 school year. That's an increase of 39 percent. The percentage of students eligible for free lunch jumped from 33 percent in 2008 when the plant was open to 50 percent in 2009 the first year it was closed.

This free lunch data does not, of course, include older Janesville residents who have no students in school, but it is a measurement that does raise concern about the future if these numbers do not improve.

A simple way to state the concern I have with school lunch data is to acknowledge the reality that 10 years after GM closed 4,543 students out of a student body of 9,735 come from homes with very modest incomes. An example of eligibility is that a family of four must have a total household income of less than $39,000 per year. Total household income might come from one, two, or maybe more jobs, and this has other consequences. The more jobs a parent has, the less time they are home being a parent.

It is also worth noting that in Janesville and elsewhere, poverty is not spread evenly across the community. Elementary schools in one part of the community have higher percentages of students eligible for free or reduced lunch than elementary schools in other parts of the community. In Janesville, it ranges from a low of 29 percent to a high of 90 percent.

8. Recovery from the loss of thousands of jobs (4,500 in the Janesville area) in a modest-sized city of 60,000 would not be overnight. Acknowledge and prepare for the fact that recovery will take time. The pain is obvious in families where they lost a GM related job. I am talking about lower-income people not directly impacted but end up feeling the impacts. This usually occurs when people who lose high-paying jobs often need to seek lower-paying jobs. It creates a domino effect. People who were making $28 per hour compete for $18 per hour jobs, driving some of those people into $12 per hour jobs and so on down the line to $7.50 per hour minimum wage jobs.

9. A community goes through a period of grief after losing a major employer. My advice to other cities that face what Janesville faced is to acknowledge these emotions. I should also mention that this all occurred in the middle of the worst national recession since the Great Depression. This double whammy was felt deeply, and ignoring it leaves many citizens devastated and confused.

10. Powerful politicians who have leverage on the corporation can sometimes help. However, there are very few of these influential people. Out of 100 senators and 435 members of Congress, there are maybe 10 to 15 of them. Does your state have one? Wisconsin did not in 2008 when GM closed the plant. It did back in the 1980s and early 1990s in Congressman Les Aspin. It had Speaker Paul Ryan from 2015 until 2018. It was bad timing that we had neither of these men in power in 2008. Ryan was a low seniority congressman in the minority party in 2008. Michigan had Congressman John Dingell.

Neither Janesville nor Wisconsin had this political power in 2008, and therefore GM was politically free to leave Janesville. Also, moving the Janesville production to Michigan and Texas meant pleasing congressional members in these two states who were more influential in Washington. The president in 2008, George W. Bush, was from Texas. Moving much of the SUV production to Texas made sense for business and political reasons.

11. Secure a solid commitment. In 1985, GM wanted a new interchange on Interstate 90 which passed Janesville and brought by truck lots of the parts needed for the assembly plant. I was the state Senate majority leader then, and with the strong support of Governor Anthony Earl, we passed legislation funding the $8 million interchange at Avalon Road and I-90. This interchange reduced the number of city streets these trucks had to use from the existing interchange exit. GM appreciated the interchange, and the plant lasted 23 more years.

GM wanted a new road in 2000 to make the route from that new interchange to the plant even more direct. Local legislators with the strong support of Governor Tommy Thompson provided the funds to pay for Reuther Way. Again, GM appreciated it but would not say the road meant any future guarantees in Janesville. Local GM management purposely did not attend the bill signing by Governor Thompson even though he came to Janesville to sign it. My former Janesville GM management sources said that Detroit GM management advised them not to come. Wow! They did not attend to avoid facing the obvious media questions about whether GM would be willing to make commitments about staying in Janesville now with the new interchange and road. They were not willing or prepared to make any commitment.

12. Janesville GM's workforce went from 7,100 in the 1970s to 3,500 in its last year. Production was about the same. The reason was technology, and specifically robots and other efficiencies negotiated by local management and UAW Local 95 in 1986. The trends in technology make it reasonable to predict that ANY relatively unskilled repetitive assembly line job can be replaced with technology. This applies across America.

13. A low unemployment rate doesn't equal a strong economy. During the 10 years since GM left Janesville, there have been numerous new jobs that have been viewed as the replacement of the lost GM jobs. But there is a considerable difference between replacing the lost GM and supplier jobs and replacing the wages and benefits that come with those jobs. This second piece has not happened, but it is bound to happen in this era of decreasing numbers of organized union workers and the increasing use of robots and other technology instead of humans.

An individual or family's inability to move to another part of the country to find a good job is commonly referred to as "immobility." Workers and their families cannot "just move." But the important question to ask is, "Where could they move to find high-paying, low-skilled assembly line jobs?" Robots are here and will inevitably become more prevalent. Robots do not need an hourly wage, health insurance, or a pension. You just need a building to put them in and a modest-sized workforce to maintain them.

14. Watch for warning signs. The more I have reflected on and researched the Janesville-GM relationship, the clearer it is that GM's commitment to Janesville was more fragile and at risk than most people realized.

The fragility was publicly seen in 1984, twenty-four years before they left for good, when GM announced that it was transferring the production of full-sized pickup trucks from Janesville to a new GM plant in Fort Wayne, Indiana. This decision cost Janesville 1,800 jobs and emptied over one-third of the plant. Almost worse was that GM Detroit was silent for over two years regarding assigning a replacement product. Silence is bad.

15. Don't be naive. Your city with a large plant owned by a large out-of-state corporation wants that corporation to care about *your* plant in *your* city. That is what we wanted in Janesville. In 2008, we learned that GM leaders in Detroit wouldn't (or couldn't) afford to care about Janesville and its workers. The entire corporation was going broke.

Large corporations do not care, and they would likely say they cannot afford to care about a particular plant and its thousands of employees and additional thousands in their families. We need to accept that corporations are not social service agencies, and contrary to the philosophy expressed by the U.S. Supreme Court's Citizens United decision, corporations are not people. If corporations are people, then why don't any of them give birth to children?

Their bottom line will always be more important than the jobs in your community. The community is at the mercy of the corporation. Accept this imbalance of power, and then do all you can to encourage them to stay. Don't give them a reason to leave.

16. A community should observe and learn that the local management of a large, out-of-state-based corporation should involve themselves as community leaders and engage in the affairs of your community. Do they serve on the council, as an alderman, or on the school board? Do they chair the United Way board or the Chamber of Commerce board? Is management encouraged to socialize with the workers? Involvement or lack of interest in these activities can tell you a lot about the company's desire to be part of the community. Remaining detached from a community makes leaving personally easier for top local management.

The answers in Janesville about the questions I raise in the above paragraph were in each case not helpful to keeping GM in Janesville. The answers were NO, NO, and NO.

17. Factory workers are not as mobile as many people with college degrees or people with skills such as firefighters, police, nurses, or teachers. If a 35- to 45-year-old factory worker loses a job, it's not easy to move to another city or state. A spouse may have a job in Janesville, their children like their school, older parents and other family members live in Janesville, they like their church. Also, where is there another $25 to $30 per hour job in manufacturing? The immobility we hear about from some "experts" ignores the "on the ground" reality of "just moving" somewhere else. To where?

18. There is an exodus of young college graduates from their hometown or home state. In my experience, I have seen this going on since the 1960s. The vast majority of my high school friends (I graduated in 1962) who went on to get college degrees did not return to Janesville, and often not even Wisconsin. The one exception I did notice was those who came home to teach. I came back to Janesville with the intention of teaching, but my career led me to politics.

19. Remember who you are and what gives your community its identity. If your community loses its major employer, it's a huge loss. But you did not lose all the other great things that made your community a great place to live and work and raise a family.

20. A community should go out and tell the world about all the positive things they still have to offer. It could be your school system, your quality of local government, your access to interstates, highways, and railroads, your cultural opportunities, local health care systems, etc. None of these assets changed because a corporation left town. **▎▎**

17

One Last Question, One Final Hope

It may be instructive to ask a hypothetical question after the closure of the Janesville GM plant after 85 years and observe the changes for GM families who lost their jobs, the impact on non-GM Janesville's economy, and the increased poverty levels in the community. Losing thousands of good paying jobs with excellent benefits was bound to contribute heavily to this situation. The national recession at the same time made it all worse.

Here is the question: If you were a Janesville citizen in 1923 and someone said to you, "You can have this GM plant here for the next 85 years. It will create a big middle class in Janesville. Employees' kids will go to college. The city will thrive economically. But then after 85 years GM will close the plant, and for at least the next 10 years the community will struggle to recover. Poverty will increase and the middle class will shrink. Would you take the deal? Would most people in Janesville take that deal?

Some people I'm sure would say yes because they would not be alive 85 years later. I assume others would think of their children, grandchildren, and great-grandchildren, who would be here in 85 years. Thinking of their descendants, would most people 85 years ago have thought the trade-off was worth it? My guess is that the majority would have taken the deal.

Were Janesville and the auto industry unique in facing these big changes? Well, no. Think of other industries that faced change and lost market share or worse: shipbuilding, steel companies, appliances, radios, tractors, clothes, shoes, farming.

The world changed and it had consequences. After all this change, we are still the wealthiest, most powerful nation in the world. New industries, through technology, were created in America. Of course, this big picture view is just that: the big picture. It is little comfort to those individuals and their families who lost their jobs.

This is an age of polarization of our politics, and it's an angry polarization unlike any time in my adult life (since 1962). What do we do about this? Some, I'm sure, don't want to do anything about it. But I do.

We need to move forward with a shared understanding of how great our country is. In the last half of the previous century, there was a broad consensus about America's greatness. We had abolished slavery; created national parks; passed laws protecting child labor; created Social Security; survived the Great Depression; defeated Hitler while winning World War II; passed the G.I. Bill; abolished segregation; increased environmental laws; created Medicare and Medicaid; acknowledged the equality of women, minorities, and people with different sexual preferences. There are other achievements I've not mentioned. There was a broad consensus on all of this, although on some issues the popular consensus did not happen overnight.

It seems today that all the above is not enough. The generation that lived through so much of it are elderly or have died. We are American. I refuse to believe that we cannot forge a new consensus. I think it should and could include much of the above.

We could start by making sure students who graduate from high school have learned about all the above. We could use modern tools, led by the internet, to find consensus opinions on issues and not even try to change political party affiliation. Maybe there is a consensus out there for the support of one word—*freedom*. Freedom means different things to different people. But there must, I believe, be a consensus on the recognition that Americans have more freedom than literally billions of people on the planet.

What is the future of good-paying jobs in America? This question deeply concerns me. People are aware of the income inequality between the very rich and the rest of America. I do not see the government seriously altering this. But I do see hope in the generosity and philosophy of some of the wealthiest Americans such as Warren Buffett and Bill and Melinda Gates in donating vast sums of their wealth to important public causes in America and across the globe. I am more optimistic about this philanthropy movement than I am in government reducing the inequality. The following quote from Francis Bacon is fitting: "Money is like manure, its only good if you spread it around."

I am also deeply concerned about another growing inequality being created by new technologies. This inequality is between the millions of Americans who are not rich but have a solid post-high school education and those who don't. The first group will end up in good family-supporting jobs, and many of them will become wealthy.

But the majority of those without learned skills through education will try to survive and support their families with two jobs and an hourly wage in 2019 dollars between $10 and $18 and limited benefits.

I will end by acknowledging the obvious. I have told the hard truth of Janesville's past and GM's history in Janesville. However, I hope people elsewhere in America will not take this as an opportunity to look down their noses at us. Janesville and GM's story of racial and gender bias are hardly an isolated situation. Who doubts that Janesville's story and GM's story in Janesville are similar to a significant number of other communities and factories in America? My hope is we are all making progress. ▪▮

ACKNOWLEDGMENTS

I wrote this book myself just like I did my first book, *Ringside Seat*, but I certainly did not do it alone. Many people were helpful with sharing details of events, dates and times, and then referring me to others who had firsthand knowledge of various events in the book. I list their names knowing that I will unintentionally leave out some people. For that I apologize.

Thanks again to Barb for supporting me on this second book. She never complained when I would go to my study to write or be off to interview someone. Many, many thanks to my stepdaughter, Erin Jacobson, who typed this entire book from my handwritten pages. My penmanship grades at St. Mary's were never high, and time has not resulted in improvement! Just like with my first book, Erin's contribution went beyond typing. She made many suggestions on changes she thought would make the document clearer. She also gave me much appreciated advice on some of the content.

The following people helped with various topics:

Bruce Penny and Terry Duller were my volunteer researchers who spent untold hours gathering documents from the UAW Hall, the Janesville Hedberg Library, the *Janesville Gazette*, and anywhere else they could go to help me find information to make this story accurate. I cannot thank them enough. As longtime GM and UAW employees, they also provided firsthand knowledge. Bruce also served as president of the UAW in the 1990s. Terry worked closely with Jim Lee during those critical years in the 1980s.

I spoke with several UAW members and leaders who were willing to share with me what they knew and observed: Mike Maerks, Dave Vaughn, Tom Brien, and the late Mike O'Brien, who I interviewed twice, including the last time about a month before his death. I had known Mike since the early 1970s. Bob McNatt and Ron Monat, both longtime friends of mine, were generous with their time and recollection of events. Bob was another Local 95 president and along with Ron went on to serve on the UAW International staff. I should also add that they both helped on my state Senate campaigns, especially the first one in 1974. Marv Wopat and Jim Conley helped as well.

Thanks to Governors Tony Earl (1983–1987), Tommy Thompson (1987–2001), and Jim Doyle (2003–2011) who spoke with me about their roles in helping keep the GM plant in Janesville.

I also had tremendous help from two former management people at GM. I believe they were completely honest with me. They insisted that they remain anonymous. I understand this. In fact, I came to believe that this insistence allowed them to be completely candid and honest. I thank them. It allowed me to write this book having both union and management perspective.

I thank John Scott III, Patricia Thom, Curt Parish, and Eric Beck for meeting with me and telling me more about their parents.

Thanks to former Janesville City Manager Phil Deaton. He is a truly honorable man.

Thanks to Greg Ardrey, a management official at Alliant Energy Corporation and longtime member of the Janesville School Board. He was born and raised in St. Louis and moved to Janesville in 1990. He is the only African American member of the Janesville School Board in at least the last 60 years, and it's likely he is the first person of his race ever to serve on the board dating back to 1839.

Thanks to Les Aspin's staff person, Ted Bornstein, who was so helpful in telling me about Aspin's role in the 1986–1989 efforts to get new products to the plant.

I owe a big thanks to Andrew Sigwell for both the photos he provided me for this book and as the third-generation owner of Zachow's, now Zoxx. He helped with the storied history of the bar and (until 1999) restaurant.

Thanks to Sue Conley and Lonnie Brigham and Janesville Police Chief Dave Moore.

There are many others whose names you will find throughout the book. I am so grateful to my editor, Doug Moe, and my publisher, Kristin Mitchell at Little Creek Press, for all their assistance. Doug, an author himself, did a terrific job on both of my books to turn this "rookie" author's work into flowing and connected books. His advice on chapter titles and chapter order were just a couple of the ways he helped. We both insisted and agreed that the final decision on content rested with me.

Finally, a very special acknowledgment to Bill Kraus: My friend who I was sure would live to be 100 or more. He tried, but we lost him on December 14, 2018, at the age of 92. He was my friend first, but he also helped me with my first book. He was a walking history book of Wisconsin government and politics from the 1950s to his last day. Bill was dedicated to honest, decent government in Wisconsin. He was the longtime chairman of the board of Common Cause Wisconsin. I had the privilege of succeeding him as chairman. Bill was also an author. He wrote *Let the People Decide*, the story of the improbable election of Lee Sherman Dreyfus as governor of Wisconsin.

I talked with Bill about this book. He had offered to read the first draft. I looked forward to his valuable input and advice. I lost my friend and that help on December 14. ⊪

BIBLIOGRAPHY

Overhaul: An Insider's Account of the Obama Administration's Emergency Rescue of the Auto Industry by Steven Rattner, 2010, published by Mariner Books/Houghton Mifflin Harcourt

Janesville: An American Story by Amy Goldstein, 2017, published by Simon and Schuster

Walter P. Reuther: Selected Papers, edited by Henry M. Christman, published by The MacMillan Co., 1961

Reuther: A Daughter Strikes by Elisabeth Reuther Dickmeyer, 1989, published by Spelman Publishers Division

Race: The Power of an Illusion. Background Readings on Science Genetics, Human Variation, Evolution, Scientific Classification, and More, http://www.pbs.org/race/000_About/002_04-background-01.htm

Life and Times of Frederick Douglas by Frederick Douglas, 1881

North Star: An abolitionist newspaper published in New Bedford, MA by Douglas (relaunched recently by Shaun King) which was named for the star followed by many escaping slaves traveling during the night toward freedom in the north.

APPENDIX

Remarks at GM plant in Janesville, Wisconsin:
"Keeping America's Promise" by Barack Obama

February 13, 2008:

It was nearly a century ago that the first tractor rolled off the assembly line at this plant. The achievement didn't just create a product to sell or profits for General Motors. It led to a shared prosperity enjoyed by all of Janesville. Homes and businesses began to sprout up along Milwaukee and Main Streets. Jobs were plentiful, with wages that could raise a family and benefits you could count on.

Prosperity hasn't always come easily. The plant shut down for a period during the height of the Depression, and major shifts in production have been required to meet the changing times. Tractors became automobiles. Automobiles became artillery shells. SUVs are becoming hybrids as we speak, and the cost of transition has always been greatest for the workers and their families.

But through hard times and good, great challenge and great change, the promise of Janesville has been the promise of America—that our prosperity can and must be the tide that lifts every boat; that we rise or fall as one nation; that our economy is strongest when our middle-class grows and opportunity is spread as widely as possible. And when it's not—when opportunity is uneven or unequal—it is our responsibility to restore balance, and fairness, and keep that promise alive for the next generation. That is the responsibility we face right now, and that is the responsibility I intend to meet as President of the United States.

We are not standing on the brink of recession due to forces beyond our control. The fallout from the housing crisis that's cost jobs and wiped out savings was not an inevitable part of the business cycle.

DISASSEMBLED

It was a failure of leadership and imagination in Washington—the culmination of decades of decisions that were made or put off without regard to the realities of a global economy and the growing inequality it's produced.

It's a Washington where George Bush hands out billions in tax cuts year after year to the biggest corporations and the wealthiest few who don't need them and don't ask for them—tax breaks that are mortgaging our children's future on a mountain of debt; tax breaks that could've gone into the pockets of the working families who needed them most.

It's a Washington where decades of trade deals like NAFTA and China have been signed with plenty of protections for corporations and their profits, but none for our environment or our workers who've seen factories shut their doors and millions of jobs disappear; workers whose right to organize and unionize has been under assault for the last eight years.

It's a Washington where politicians like John McCain and Hillary Clinton voted for a war in Iraq that should've never been authorized and never been waged—a war that is costing us thousands of precious lives and billions of dollars a week that could've been used to rebuild crumbling schools and bridges; roads and buildings; that could've been invested in job training and child care; in making health care affordable or putting college within reach.

And it's a Washington that has thrown open its doors to lobbyists and special interests who've riddled our tax code with loopholes that let corporations avoid paying their taxes while you're paying more. They've been allowed to write an energy policy that's keeping us addicted to oil when there are families choosing between gas and groceries. They've used money and influence to kill health care reform at a time when half of all bankruptcies are caused by medical bills, and then they've rigged our bankruptcy laws to make it harder to climb out of debt. They don't represent ordinary Americans, they don't fund my campaign, and they won't drown out the voices of working families when I am President.

This is what's been happening in Washington at a time when we have greater income disparity in this country than we've seen since the first year of the Great Depression. At a time when some CEOs are making more in a day than the average workers makes in a year. When the typical family income has dropped by $1,000 over the last seven years. When wages are flat, jobs are moving overseas, and we've never paid more for health care, or energy, or college. It's a time when we've never saved less—barely $400 for the average family last year—and never owed more—an average of $8,000 per family. And it's a time when one in eight Americans now lives in abject poverty right here in the richest nation on Earth.

At a time like this, it's no wonder that the mortgage crisis was the straw that broke the camel's back. The equity that people own in their homes is often their largest source of savings, and as millions upon millions have seen those savings and their home equity decline or disappear altogether, so have their dreams for a better future.

I realize that politicians come before you every election saying that they'll change all this. They lay out big plans and hold events with workers just like this one, because it's popular to do and it's easy to make promises in the heat of a campaign.

But how many times have you been disappointed when everyone goes back to Washington and nothing changes? Because the lobbyists just write another check. Or because politicians start worrying about how they'll win the next election instead of why they should. Because they're focused on who's up and who's down instead of who matters— the worker who just lost his pension; the family that just put up the

For Sale sign; the young woman who gets three hours of sleep a night because she works the late shift after a full day of college and still can't afford her sister's medicine.

These are the Americans who need real change—the kind of change that's about more than switching the party in the White House. They need a change in our politics—a leader who can end the division in Washington so we can stop talking about our challenges and start solving them; who doesn't defend lobbyists as part of the system, but sees them as part of the problem; who will carry your voices and your hopes into the White House every single day for the next four years. And that is the kind of President I want to be.

I didn't spend my career in the halls of Washington, I began it in the shadow of a closed steel mill on the South Side of Chicago. We organized churches and community leaders; African-Americans, whites, and Hispanics to lift neighborhoods out of poverty; provide job training to the jobless; and set up after school programs so that kids had a safe place to go while their parents worked.

Those are the voices I carried with me to the Illinois state Senate, where I brought Democrats and Republicans together to expand health insurance to 150,000 children and parents; where I led the fight to provide $100 million in tax relief for working families and the working poor.

They're the voices I carried with me to Washington, where the first bill I introduced was to make college more affordable; where I fought against a bankruptcy bill that made it harder for families to climb out of debt; and where I passed the most sweeping lobbying reform in a generation—reform that forced lobbyists to tell the American people who they're raising money from and who in Congress they're funneling it to.

So when I talk about real change that will make a real difference in the lives of working families—change that will restore balance in our economy and put us on a path to prosperity—it's not just the poll-tested rhetoric of a political campaign. It's the cause of my life. And you can be sure that it will be the cause of my presidency from the very first day I take office.

Now we know that we cannot put up walls around our economy. We know that we cannot reverse the tide of technology that's allowed businesses to send jobs wherever there's an internet connection. We know that government cannot solve all our problems, and we don't expect it to.

But that doesn't mean we have to accept an America of lost opportunity and diminished dreams. Not when we still have the most productive, highly-educated, best-skilled workers in the world. Not when we still stand on the cutting edge of innovation, and science, and discovery. Not when we have the resources and the will of a decent, generous people who are ready to share in the burdens and benefits of a global economy. I am certain that we can keep America's promise—for this generation and the next.

So today, I'm laying out a comprehensive agenda to reclaim our dream and restore our prosperity. It's an agenda that focuses on three broad economic challenges that the next President must address—the current housing crisis; the cost crisis facing the middle-class and those struggling to join it; and the need to create millions of good jobs right here in America- jobs that can't be outsourced and won't disappear.

The first challenge is to stem the fallout from the housing crisis and put in place rules of the road to prevent it from happening again.

A few weeks ago I offered an economic stimulus package based on a simple principle—we should get immediate relief into the hands of people who need it the most and will spend it the quickest. I proposed *sending each working family a $500 tax cut and each senior a $250 supplement to their Social Security check. And if the economy gets worse, we should double those amounts.*

Neither George Bush nor Hillary Clinton had that kind of immediate, broad-based relief in their original stimulus proposals, but I'm glad that the stimulus package that was recently passed by Congress does. We still need to go further, though, and make unemployment insurance available for a longer period of time and for more Americans who find themselves out of work. We should also provide assistance to state and local governments so that they don't slash critical services like health care or education.

For those Americans who are facing the brunt of the housing crisis, I've proposed a fund that would provide direct relief to victims of mortgage fraud. We'd also help those who are facing closure refinance their mortgages so they can stay in their homes. And I'd provide struggling homeowners relief by offering a tax credit to low- and middle-income Americans that would cover ten percent of their mortgage interest payment every year.

To make sure that folks aren't tricked into purchasing loans they can't afford, I've proposed tough new penalties for those who commit mortgage fraud, and a Home Score system that would allow consumers to compare various mortgage products so that they can find out whether or not they'll be able to afford the payments ahead of time.

The second major economic challenge we have to address is the cost crisis facing the middle-class and the working poor. As the housing crisis spills over into other parts of the economy, we've seen people's entire life savings wiped out in an instant. It's the result of skyrocketing costs, stagnant wages, and disappearing benefits that are pushing more and more Americans towards a debt spiral from which they can't escape. We have to give them a way out by cutting costs, putting more money in their pockets, and rebuilding a safety net that's become badly frayed over the last decades.

One of the principles that John Edwards has passionately advanced is that this country should be rewarding work, not wealth. That starts with our tax code, which has been rigged by lobbyists with page after page of loopholes that benefit big corporations and the wealthiest few. For example, we should not be giving tax breaks to corporations that make their profits in some other country with some other workers. Before she started running for President, Senator Clinton actually voted for this loophole.

I'll change our tax code so that it's simple, fair, and advances opportunity, not the agenda of some lobbyist. I am the only candidate in this race who's proposed a genuine middle-class tax cut that will provide relief to 95% of working Americans. This is a tax cut -paid for in part by closing corporate loopholes and shutting down tax havens—that will offset the payroll tax that working Americans are already paying, and it'll be worth up to $1000 for a working family. We'll also eliminate income taxes for any retiree making less than $50,000 per year, because our seniors are struggling enough with rising costs, and should be able to retire in dignity and respect. Since the Earned Income Tax Credit lifts nearly 5 million Americans out of poverty each year, I'll double the number of workers who receive it and triple the benefit for minimum wage workers. And I won't wait another ten years to raise the minimum wage—I'll guarantee that it keeps pace with inflation every single year so that it's not just a minimum wage, but a living wage. Because that's the change that working Americans need.

My universal health care plan brings down the cost of health care more than any other candidate in this race, and will save the typical family up to $2500 a year on their premiums. Every American would be able to get the same kind of health care that members of Congress get for themselves, and we'd ban insurance companies from denying you coverage because of a pre-existing condition. And the main difference between my plan and Senator Clinton's plan is that she'd require the government to force you to buy health insurance and she said she'd "go after" your wages if you don't. Well I believe the reason people don't have health care isn't because no one's forced them to buy it, it's because no one's made it affordable—and that's what we'll do when I am President.

If we want to train our workforce for a knowledge economy, it's also time that we brought down the cost of a college education and put it within reach of every American. I know how expense this is. At the beginning of our marriage, Michelle and I were spending more to payoff our college loans than we were on our mortgage. So I'll create a new and fully refundable tax credit worth $4,000 for tuition and fees every year, a benefit that students will get in exchange for community or national service, which will cover two-thirds of the tuition at the average public college or university. And I'll also simplify the financial aid application process so that we don't have a million students who aren't applying for aid because it's too difficult.

With so many mothers and fathers juggling work and parenting, the next cost we have to bring down is the cost of living in a two-income family. I'll expand the child care tax credit for people earning less than $50,000 a year, and I'll double spending on quality afterschool programs. We'll also expand the Family Medical Leave Act to include more businesses and millions more workers; and we'll change a system that's stacked against working women by requiring every employer to provide seven paid sick days a year, so that you can be home with your child if they're sick.

In addition to cutting costs for working families, we also need to help them save more—especially for retirement. That's why we'll require employers to enroll every worker in a direct deposit retirement account that places a small percentage of each paycheck into savings. You can keep this account even if you change jobs, and the federal government will match the savings for lower-income, working families.

Finally, we need to help families who find themselves in a debt spiral climb out. Since so many who are struggling to keep up with their mortgages are now shifting their debt to credit cards, we have to make sure that credit cards don't become the next stage in the housing crisis. To make sure that Americans know what they're signing up for, I'll institute a five-star rating system to inform consumers about the level of risk involved in every credit card. And we'll establish a Credit Card Bill of Rights that will ban unilateral changes to a credit card agreement; ban rate changes to debt that's already incurred; and ban interest on late fees. Americans need to pay what they owe, but they should pay what's fair, not what fattens profits for some credit card company.

The same principle should apply to our bankruptcy laws. When I first arrived in the Senate, I opposed the credit card industry's bankruptcy bill that made it harder for working families to climb out of debt. Five years earlier, Senator Clinton had supported a nearly identical bill. And during a debate a few weeks back, she said that even though she voted for it, she was glad it didn't pass. Now, I know those kind of antics might make sense in Washington, but they don't make much sense anywhere else, and they certainly don't make sense for working families who are struggling under the weight of their debt.

When I'm President, we'll reform our bankruptcy laws so that we give Americans who find themselves in debt a second chance. I'll close the loophole that allows investors with multiple homes to renegotiate their mortgage in bankruptcy court, but not victims of predatory lending. We'll make sure that if you can demonstrate that you went bankrupt because of medical expenses, then you can relieve that debt and get back on your feet. And I'll make sure that CEOs can't dump your pension with one hand while they collect a bonus with the other. That's an outrage, and it's time we had a President who knows it's an outrage.

Those are the steps we can take to ease the cost crisis facing working families. But we still need to make sure that families are working. We need to maintain our competitive edge in a global by ensuring that plants like this one stay open for another hundred years, and shuttered factories re-open as new industries that promise new jobs. And we need to put more Americans to work doing jobs that need to be done right here in America.

For years, we have stood by while our national infrastructure has crumbled and decayed. In 2005, the American Society of Civil Engineers gave it a D, citing problems with our airports, dams, schools, highways, and waterways. One out of three urban bridges were classified as structurally deficient, and we all saw the tragic results of what that could mean in Minnesota last year. Right here in Wisconsin, we know that $500 million of freight will come through this state by 2020, and if we do not have the infrastructure to handle it, we will not get the business.

For our economy, our safety, and our workers, we have to rebuild America. I'm proposing a National Infrastructure Reinvestment Bank that will invest $60 billion over ten years. This investment will multiply into almost half a trillion dollars of additional infrastructure spending and generate nearly two million new jobs—many of them in the construction industry that's been hard hit by this housing crisis. The repairs will be determined not by politics, but by what will maximize our safety and homeland security; what will keep our environment clean and our economy strong. And we'll fund this bank by ending this war in Iraq. It's time to stop spending billions of dollars a week trying to put Iraq back together and start spending the money on putting America back together instead.

It's also time to look to the future and figure out how to make trade work for American workers. I won't stand here and tell you that we can—or should—stop free trade. We can't stop every job from going overseas. But I also won't stand here and accept an America where we do nothing to help American workers who have lost jobs and opportunities because of these trade agreements. And that's a position of mine that doesn't change based on who I'm talking to or the election I'm running in.

You know, in the years after her husband signed NAFTA, Senator Clinton would go around talking about how great it was and how many benefits it would bring. Now that she's running for President, she says we need a time-out on trade. No one knows when this time-out will end. Maybe after the election.

I don't know about a time-out, but I do know this—when I am President, I will not sign another trade agreement unless it has protections for our environment and protections for American workers. And I'll pass the Patriot Employer Act that I've been fighting for ever since I ran for the Senate—we will end the tax breaks for companies who ship our jobs overseas, and we will give those breaks to companies who create good jobs with decent wages right here in America.

I believe that we can create millions of those jobs around a clean, renewable energy future. A few hours northeast of here is the city of Manitowoc. For over a century, it was the home of Mirro manufacturing—a company that provided thousands of jobs and plenty of business. In 2003, Mirro closed its doors for good after losing thousands of jobs to Mexico.

But in the last few years, something extraordinary has happened.

Thanks to the leadership of Governor Doyle and Mayor Kevin Crawford, Manitowoc has re-trained its workers and attracted new businesses and new jobs. Orion Energy Systems works with companies to reduce their electricity use and carbon emissions. And Tower Tech is now making wind turbines that are being sold all over the world. Hundreds of people have found new work, and unemployment has been cut in half.

This can be America's future. I know that General Motors received some bad news yesterday, and I know how hard your Governor has fought to keep jobs in this plant. But I also know how much progress you've made—how many hybrids and fuel-efficient vehicles you're churning out. And I believe that if our government is there to support you, and give you the assistance you need to re-tool and make this transition, that this plant will be here for another hundred years. The question is not whether a clean energy economy is in our future, it's where it will thrive. I want it to thrive right here in the United States of America; right here in Wisconsin; and that's the future I'll fight for as your President.

My energy plan will invest $150 billion over ten years to establish a green energy sector that will create up to 5 million new jobs over the next two decades—jobs that pay well and can't be outsourced. We'll also provide funding to help manufacturers convert to green technology and help workers learn the skills they need for these jobs.

We know that all of this must be done in a responsible way, without adding to the already obscene debt that has grown by four trillion dollars under George Bush. We know that we cannot build our future on a credit card issued by the bank of China. And that is why I've paid for every element of this economic agenda—by ending a war that's costing us billions, closing tax loopholes for corporations, putting a price on carbon pollution, and ending George Bush's tax cuts for the wealthiest 2% of Americans.

In the end, this economic agenda won't just require new money. It will require a new spirit of cooperation and innovation on behalf of the American people. We will have to learn more, and study more, and work harder. We'll be called upon to take part in shared sacrifice and shared prosperity. And we'll have to remind ourselves that we rise and fall as one nation; that a country in which only a few prosper is antithetical to our ideals and our democracy; and that those of us who have benefited greatly from the blessings of this country have a solemn obligation to open the doors of opportunity, not just for our children, but to all of America's children.

That is the spirit that's thrived in Janesville from the moment that first tractor came off the assembly line so many years ago. It's the spirit that led my grandmother to her own assembly line during World War II, and my grandfather to march in Patton's Army. When that war ended, they were given the chance to go to college on the GI Bill, to buy a house from the Federal Housing Authority, and to give my mother the chance to go to the best schools and dream as big as the Kansas sky. Even though she was a single mom who didn't have much, it's the same chance she gave me, and why I'm standing here today.

It's a promise that's been passed down through the ages; one that each generation of Americans is called to keep—that we can raise our children in a land of boundless opportunity, broad prosperity, and unyielding possibility. That is the promise we must keep in our time, and I look forward to working and fighting to make it real as President of the United States. Thank you.

Excerpts from August, 1976 John Scott interview conducted by Clem Inhoff of the Wisconsin State Historical Society as part of their bicentennial project:

- Answer: "Well, a black person would have to buy a house if he wanted live in Janesville at the time that I came here. And oh, on—the first little house was just east of the Wilson School that I was interested in, which was $3500. And I was asked to ask some of the neighbors in that neighborhood if they cared if I lived in that neighborhood."

- Answer: "So anyway, well, I went to three of four houses and knocked on the door, and come to find out that they were railroad man too. Some worked for the Chicago & Northwestern, some worked for the Milwaukee Road. And we set there—we had—they didn't look at my color, and we had—I had coffee and donuts or coffee and cookies. And we just set there and talked as if we had known each other all our lives. They said, 'Well, what's the difference if you are colored, or if you are a negro?' Said, 'You're a human just like we—just like we are. We are—just as good as we are."

- Answer: "(a neighbor said) 'If you feel like you ought to live here in Janesville, you have as much right to live here in Janesville as anybody else.' Well, I didn't go any further after contacting those four housewives."

- Question: "Well, how did—how did you come to know that you had to buy if you wanted to live here?"

- Answer: "Well, because when my wife and I first came here, the—we couldn't get a room at a hotel overnight. We were promised a room at the Milner Hotel, through the police department. He called. They tried to help us out. So when we went to the Milner Hotel, and this man saw that we were colored, he said the room was just rented. I said, 'But you said you would—you promised this sergeant at the police station you would save the room for us.' He said, 'Well,' he said, 'First come, first served.' So I said, 'Thank you.' So I went out—my wife and I, we left. We went back over to the police station and told them just what this clerk had told me at the—at the Milner Hotel. And so then he called—made a call over across town, which is up near—near town, about a room there. And this person said, 'Why sure,' said, 'I have rooms here,' but—she had transients. So he said, 'Well,' he said, 'they are colored.' She said, 'Don't make any difference if they are. Send them on up here.' So we went up there. And that place, now, is located at 104 South Locust. So we went there. She was a widow woman, and she was very il that night when we got there. Matter of fact, she was so ill that she couldn't go up the stairway. She was sitting in the kitchen. She suffered asthma awfully bad. So we went up the stairway. She told us where to find our room, so we went into our room, so we closed the door, we went to bed. And the next morning we met a couple other ladies who was rooming there, and they was very nice and friendly, spoke to us with a nice smile."

- Answer: "So coming out of that—coming out of Chicago that evening, the same couple was on the train. And after the rush hour between Chicago and Woodstock, well, then I had a little time to sit down with this couple again. And it just so happened that they were—went to—they were down at the racetracks, and he had a—pretty good luck down there at the racetracks. And this—this husband asked me, I said—'John, how many children do you have?' I said, 'Three.' Well, I can't recall—he said, 'Well,' he said, 'we had pretty good luck at the racetracks today.' He said, 'Here's some money for the children, to take home to the kids.' I don't remember now just now much it was, but it was a very nice little gift. So as the kid has the piggy banks in quart fruit jars, I thanked him for the money, and I told him I would—certainly he could depend on me putting it in the kids' piggy banks. And so got acquainted. It was just like we were old friends, just like we had known each other for years. So on my trip back into Chicago that Sunday, well, when I went home, well, I took this money out and I put it in these quart jars, divided it up among the three children in these quart jars, just as I had promised. And after they, the children, had got so much in their piggy banks, well, then I took the money down to the Morgan Park Post Office and took out war bonds. So then I began to talk to my wife about Janesville, and I told her I'd take a look around Janesville. When I got my layover, which was ten days, then it'd give me time to look around over at Janesville. And in my next trip I came back to look around. Then I visited schools, and I met Mr. Williams and some of the other teachers there, and there I was—was well accepted there at the schools. The teachers were very nice. Mr. Williams took me around visiting, touring the school, and introduced me to the teachers. And I—I was really impressed about this school and the conditions of the school there, and I thought that that would be a very nice—Janesville would be a very nice place to live in order to bring my children up, to give them the proper education. And not having—at least I did, that there were no colored people here, I had not even given that a thought. But after coming to Janesville and finding that there were no colored people here, only two, three colored families, the George Davis family, the Ike Williams family, and the Enlow (phonetic) family, but still that did not bother me any at all because I had been around white people, I would say, practically 70 percent of my life, and I found no problems being around and living around with them in mixed neighborhoods. I had no trouble with them, and I felt that i could live right here in Janesville with them without any problems also."

- Question: "Now, you—you don't seem to have any recollections of discrimination connected with your work with the—with the C&NW. Or am I assuming too much here?"

- Answer: "No, there was no—no, I didn't run into any discrimination. No, I didn't run into any discrimination."

- Answer: "And I think that the colored people that come to Janesville, I think they should take more interest in the churches here in Janesville, since they are living here, and this is their community. And if they want to get acquainted with the people here and find out just how the people are here, and how they are to live with and get along with, then they should join these churches and get acquainted. That's the way we had to do. And regardless of whether it was Janesville or anyplace else, if you expect to become a part of these people and a part of their community, you're going to have to work with these people and join their organizations, join their churches. And that is your first start, is getting acquainted with the school faculty and your church and its members. There's your start right there."

- Question: "Did—did you experience, or your family experience any forms of discrimination that you recall after moving here in '48?"

- Answer: "So anyway, I attended this show, and so after the show we were all going out one night. Oh, we (coworkers) just thought we'd just go out and have a beer, and so I went out with the bunch. And we had one fellow there was from Missouri. He was a World War II—World War II veteran. And so we went out here to a tavern called the Brown Derby. So we went out there, we—I think we'd had a couple rounds of beer, and I was going to order a round of beer when the owner walked out, and he told the bartender not to serve us anything. And this mechanic looked at him—well, they were—they knew each other, and—and in the army together. So this fellow that owned the Brown Derby—I learned later he was from Tennessee, and he didn't want to serve colored people in there. So anyway, so this mechanic, he just told him off good, and just told him—you know, he kind of swore a little bit, and told him, he said, 'If Scotty isn't good enough to drink in here,' he said, 'we are not good enough to drink in here either.'"

- Answer: "So anyway, well, if you would look at Al, well, he has a sort of a foreign complexion, and he don't have kinky hair. And matter of fact, Al could say that he's any kind of a minority—minority race, and get by with it. He has that kind of complexion."

- Question: "Now, who did he blame for the loss of his job?"

- Answer: "Well, he'd never say where he blamed anybody. Al was just one of those kind of a guy that he just don't go around complaining. He's not a trouble-maker. He tried to—thething of it is, I learned about Al, he's just a hard worker, and I guess he just feel, 'Well, I can't make it here, I'll make it someplace else.'

- Question: "Now, so as far as your getting the work at the job at General Motors, it was through a Masonic connection?"

- Answer: "Two—"

- Question: "But you can't be more specific than that?"

- Answer: "No."

- Answer: "Sure, I knew the score."

- Question: "What do you mean?"

- Answer: "I knew that they had a discriminated contract there, but not with the national. But I did know that they had a local discriminated contract there. And that's why I wasn't hired, because General Motors and Fisher Body had colored employees throughout the United States. Everywhere they had a plant, they had a colored—they had colored employees. But here I was—I was just very much surprised to come here to find out that they wouldn't hire colored people at this plant."

- Answer: "Elmer Yenney, he got a little bit nasty. That was the one and only time that I really have been insulted here in Janesville."

- Question: "What did he do or say?"

- Answer: "He said, 'As long as I am president of Local No. 121, there will never be any of your kind here. To me, you are just another Paul Robeson.' So I look at him. I was a good man. We walked out the door together. He was going to lunch. And I look at that mab, and I looked at his clothes, and I said to myself, 'You might be a white man, and you might be president of Local No. 121, but I'm not as dirty and filthy as you are."

- Answer: "I said, 'Well, I don't know.' I said, 'They just tell me that they're not hiring.' He said but I could come back every six months because they throw the old applications out and take in new applications."

- Question: "Now, what, just exactly, was the nature of your work with GM when you did begin—begin work there?

- Answer: "So anyway, I started out that evening and I just—just in a matter of time of—I was on my own. So my foreman,

Ryan, came to me and he says, 'Scotty,' he said, 'we have been watching you,' said, 'you're really doing a good job.' He said, 'We are going to start you out from 4:30 with top wages with the rest of them.' He said, 'Instead of waiting say, for your sixty-days five-cent raise after sixty days, and then your six-months, right where you was supposed to get the other five cents,' said, 'you start out with the rest, paid as the older ones get,' said, 'because you just picked this job right up, and you're on your own.' So therefore, when I got my paycheck, my paycheck was the same as the others'."

• Answer: "Some of them just sitting over there looking at me, and I remember a fellow there by the name of Bell. I think he was a custodian, but his name is Bell. He's retired now. I see him once in a while up here at the clinic. Anyway, well, he had taken a liking to me. He'd always come by, and he'd always have a word or so for me. And matter of fact, all of them there, they began to talk, you no and have—always have a good word for me. So, oh, it went on some time. I got along just fine there. And finally one day I went in there, there was a new job opening up, and my foreman, Pete Glass, came over and asked me if I would like to have the job over there steaming head liners. So he said, 'It's a better job than this.' So I said, 'Well,' I said, 'I'll try it out,' I said, 'and see if I can make it.' So he took me up on this job and he broke me in on the head liners." ▮

DISASSEMBLED